FRETBOARD FORENSICS SERIES ™

# The Little Guitar Book That Could

## Tenth Position

by

Walter Klosowski III

is published exclusively through:

OMP®
OMNI MUSIC PRESS

OMNI MUSIC PRESS ®
7308 E 68th Pl Tulsa, OK 74133

http://www.omnimusicpress.com

Written, designed, edited, compiled, printed & distributed by the author.

Order Number OMP 003-010

ISBN 978-0578596815     Library of Congress Control Number: 2020921236

# The Little Guitar Book That Could

## TENTH POSITION

Walter Klosowski III

**OMP®**
OMNI MUSIC PRESS

This book is dedicated to Heath Brian Chesney, a fine guitarist outright, but also one that challenged you into becoming a better player. More importantly, he understood very well just how music connects to, or relates to, other people. Once, while listening to guitarist Jimmy Bruno, Heath told me out of the blue, "If Conan the Barbarian had iTunes, Iron Maiden would certainly be on it." See what I mean?

# THE LITTLE GUITAR BOOK THAT COULD...

... SHOWCASES THE GUITAR'S C A G E D CHORD AND SCALE SEQUENCE EXCLUSIVELY IN THE TENTH POSITION FOR EVERY ONE TO SEE, USE AND REFERENCE. THIS DETAILED *LITTLE GUITAR BOOK THAT COULD* DOES PRESUME THE FOLLOWING:

1) GUITAR POSITION DETAIL —

THERE IS A STRAIGHTFORWARD, EXPLICIT SIX CONSECUTIVE FRET AREA THAT DELINEATES THE TENTH POSITION, AND IT SPANS TWO OCTAVES PLUS A PERFECT FOURTH...

2) FRETTING HAND DETAIL —

IN GENERAL, THE SECOND AND THIRD FINGERS STAY FIXED IN THEIR RESPECTIVE FRETS, FOR NOW, AS THE FIRST AND FOURTH FINGERS STRETCH...

3) PICKING HAND DETAIL —

A NOTEWORTHY "(①E$^3$ –③G$^3$ –⑤A$^3$ –②C$^{1-4}$ –④D$^3$ –⑥E$^3$)" PICKING PATTERN OCCURS AS THE C A G E D ROOT NOTE SEQUENCE IS PLUCKED ALPHABETICALLY...

## 4) MAIN ROOT NOTE DETAIL —

The term "MAIN ROOT NOTES" characterizes the roots that usually cluster beneath the second and third fingers. However, in the tenth position, the C MAIN ROOT NOTE(S) employ the first and fourth finger(s), making it an exception here...

## 5) OCTAVE DETAIL —

The interval between one musical pitch and another with half or double its own frequency is a perfect octave. In guitarland, octaves are frequently "one string one fret away". Otherwise, two strings and or two frets are involved...

## 6) UNISON DETAIL —

When a pair or more of notes sound the same pitch it is said they are in unison. And in guitarland, it usually means "same note different string or fret". It's a practical given that the unison itself occurs in the position at hand...

7) ②ND④TH, 1ST & 4TH –

SHORTHAND FOR THE ②ND④TH STRING(S), 1ST & 4TH
FINGER(S) **MAIN** C ROOT NOTE(S) OR "DOT(S)"...

8) ⑤TH, 3RD –

SHORTHAND FOR THE ⑤TH STRING, 3RD FINGER **MAIN** A
ROOT NOTE OR "DOT"; ANCHORING THE A MATERIAL...

9) ③RD, 3RD –

SHORTHAND FOR THE ③RD STRING, 3RD FINGER **MAIN** G
ROOT NOTE OR "DOT"; ANCHORING THE G MATERIAL...

10) ①ST⑥TH, 3RD –

SHORTHAND FOR THE ①ST⑥TH STRING(S), 3RD FINGER
**MAIN** E ROOT NOTE(S) OR "DOT(S)"; ANCHORING E...

11) ④TH, 3RD –

SHORTHAND FOR THE ④TH STRING, 3RD FINGER **MAIN** D
ROOT NOTE OR "DOT"; ANCHORING THE D MATERIAL...

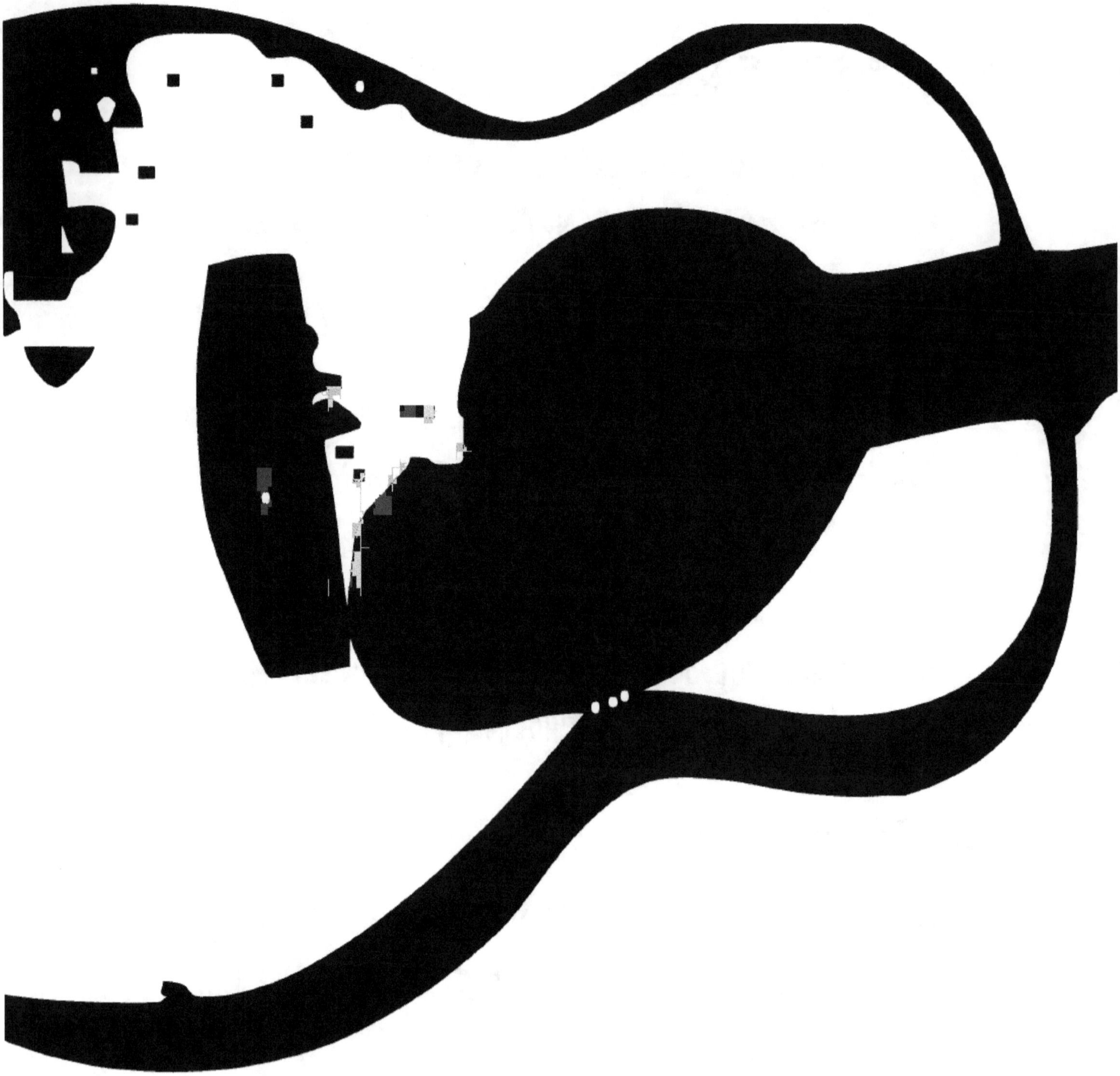

# TABLE OF CONTENTS

# TABLE OF CONTENTS ...

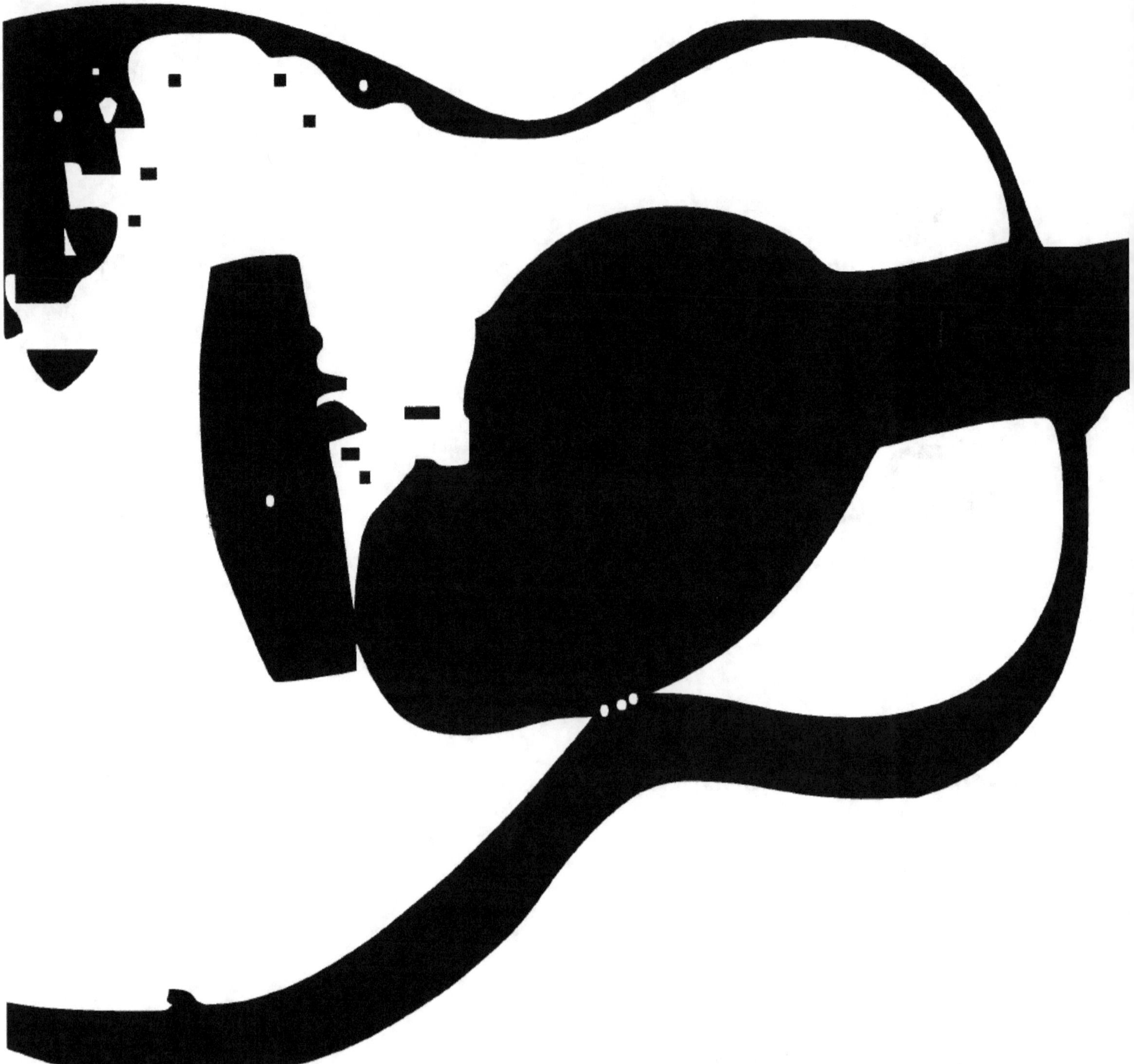

# Tenth Position Preface

Fret

*10*

(First String)

(Second String)

(Third String)

(Fourth String)

(Fifth String)

(Sixth String)

E

C

G

D

A

E

C

① ② ③ ④ ⑤ ⑥

1- 1 **2 3** 4- 4

Fingers

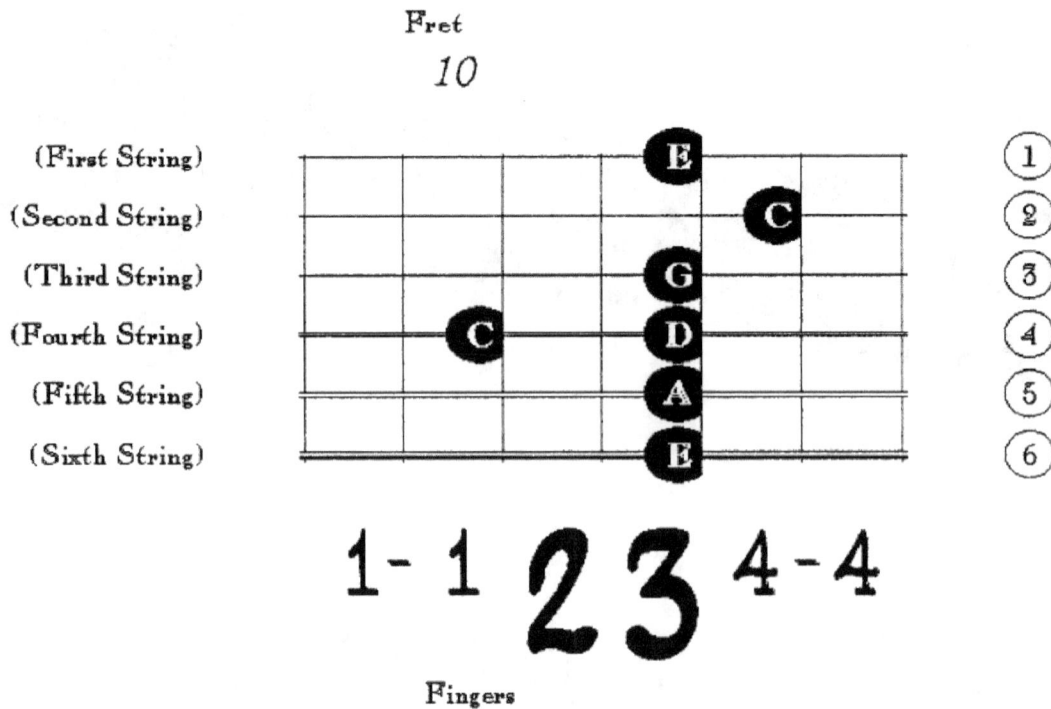

THIS GRID REPRESENTS THE GUITAR'S TENTH POSITION AS FOUND IN THIS BOOK. THE THINNEST STRING IS ON TOP, AND IT HAS SIX CONSECUTIVE FRETS. THE FOUR FINGERS ON THE FRETTING HAND CENTER THEMSELVES INSIDE THE SIX FRETS, ONE FINGER PER, LEAVING AN EMPTY FRET ON EACH SIDE. THE SECOND AND THIRD FINGERS NOW FUNCTION AS A UNIT, FIXED IN THE HEART OF THE POSITION ITSELF. THIS STATIONARY ATTRIBUTE IS WHAT ALLOWS THE FIRST AND FOURTH FINGERS TO STRETCH TO THE NOTES IN THEIR OUTER FRET AREAS. THE NOTES UNDER THE SECOND AND THIRD FINGERS ARE DUBBED **MAIN** ROOT NOTES, AND IN THIS POSITION MOST FALL BENEATH THE THIRD FINGER; THAT

FINGER FRETTING. THE SECOND FINGER IS NOT USED, BUT
IS TYPICALLY EMPLOYED. ALSO NOTICE THE EXCEPTION, AS
EITHER C **MAIN** ROOT NOTE(S) HERE EMPLOY THE FIRST AND
THE FOURTH FINGERS, RESPECTIVELY. THE EXAMPLE BELOW
OFFERS FURTHER CLARITY.

TENTH GUITAR POSITION, FINGERING DETAIL, COMPLETE WITH STRETCHES
   10TH FRET
   1-1 2 3 4-4
   ⬤   POSITION NUMBER BEHIND SECOND FINGER, ONE FINGER PER FRET [1]

IN GUITARLAND, IT'S THE FRET NUMBER BEHIND THE SECOND
FINGER, WHERE THE FIRST FINGER TYPICALLY RESIDES, THAT
ASCERTAINS THE POSITION'S LOCALE; NOT THE INDEX FINGER
IN AND OF ITSELF. THIS MAY CLARIFY WHY IT'S IMPORTANT
TO KEEP THE SECOND AND THIRD FINGERS WHERE THEY ARE,
FOR NOW, HOVERING IN THEIR FRETS. THEY DON'T STRETCH
AND THERE ISN'T A SPACE BETWEEN THEM. THAT SAID, THE
NOTES FOUND THERE ARE IMPORTANT AND TAUGHT PRIOR TO
ANY OF THE OTHERS. ONCE MEMORIZED, THE FOCUS SHIFTS
TO THEIR MATCHING OCTAVES AS FOUND IN THE OUTER FRET
AREAS, THIS ROUNDING OUT THE FRAMEWORK AS DISCUSSED.
LAST, THIS POSITION SPANS TWO OCTAVES PLUS A PERFECT
FOURTH, IF THE GUITAR REMAINS IN STANDARD TUNING.

[1] MICK GOODRICK. THE ADVANCING GUITARIST. APPLYING GUITAR CONCEPTS & TECHNIQUES. MILWAUKEE, WI. HAL LEONARD MUSIC PUBLISHING. 1987. PAGES 27-29

THESE ARE THE FOUR CHORD TYPES PRESENTED IN THIS BOOK.  THE ROWS PROVIDE ALTERNATE VOICING CHOICE.

| Augmented | Major | Minor | Diminished |
|---|---|---|---|
| | | | |
| 1 2 3 4 | 1 2 3 4 | 1 2 3 4 | 1 2 3 4 |
| | | | |
| 1 2 3 4 | 1 2 3 4 | 1 2 3 4 | 1 2 3 4 |

DO UNDERSTAND THAT THE CHORD SEQUENCE PRESENTED IS DELIBERATE SUCH THAT AS THE EYES TRAVERSE THE IMAGES FROM LEFT TO RIGHT, OR VISE VERSA, ONLY ONE NOTE WILL BE ALTERED OR CHANGED.  OBSERVE THE AUGMENTED CHORD BEGINS AS IT MORPHS OVER TO MAJOR, THE FIFTH IN FLUX. AS THE MAJOR CHORD FOLLOWS, IT THEN MORPHS TO MINOR WITH THE ALTERED THIRD.  IT ENDS WITH THE MINOR CHORD MORPHING OVER TO THE DIMINISHED VIA THE ALTERED FIFTH. PLACING THE CHORD MATERIAL IN THIS LIGHT LEAVES LITTLE TO CHANCE ENHANCING ITS MEMORIZATION.  THE GRIDS ATOP THE PAGE DETAIL THE CHORD TYPE; ANY RELATED MATERIAL, SUCH AS DOMINANT SEVENTH, IS PLACED BENEATH.

## Augmented chord — (brings musical tension)

This chord type consists of one major third interval with yet another major third interval placed on top. From the root, it's a major third with an augmented fifth. The dominant seventh brings tension as well.

## Major chord — (brings musical stability)

This chord type consists of one major third interval with one minor third interval stacked on top. From the root, it's a major third interval; but now with a perfect fifth.

## Minor chord — (brings musical stability)

This chord type consists of one minor third interval with one major third interval stacked on top. From the root, it's a minor third interval with the familiar perfect fifth as is.

## Diminished chord — (brings musical tension)

This unavoidable chord type consists of a minor third interval with another minor third interval stacked on top. Given, it's a minor third with a diminished fifth.

These are the four scale types presented in this book.  The rows provide alternate voicing choice.

| Melodic Descending | Harmonic | Melodic Ascending | Major |
|---|---|---|---|
| 1 2 3 4 | 1 2 3 4 | 1 2 3 4 | 1 2 3 4 |
| 1 2 3 4 | 1 2 3 4 | 1 2 3 4 | 1 2 3 4 |

When the eyes traverse the scales left to right, or otherwise, only one note will be altered or changed. Look to see; as the melodic minor descending morphs to the harmonic, only the seventh scale degree will change.  From there, as the harmonic minor morphs to the melodic minor ascending (or jazz minor) only the sixth scale degree will change.  Last, as the melodic minor ascending morphs to the major scale, only the third scale degree will change.  Deliberately putting the material in this light simplifies its learning.  The grid row atop details the scale; any related material such as the minor pentatonic is placed beneath.

## Melodic minor scale descending form

This scale variety is identical to the aeolian, natural or pure minor. The minor pentatonic scale is likewise derived from it. The very useful "three on a string" minor pentatonic is placed beneath the melodic minor.

## Harmonic minor scale

This scale type is the traditional minor scale taught in the various music textbooks, scholarly references and methods. It is usually presented as opposite to that of the more blissful sounding major scale.

## Melodic minor scale ascending form

This scale type is also recognized as the jazz minor scale. It is typically presented as corresponding to the descending melodic minor previously discussed.

## Major scale

This scale type is most significant. All of the major keys, all of the minor keys, and all of the modes are based on it. It's routinely used when demonstrating and or conveying other musical criteria as well.

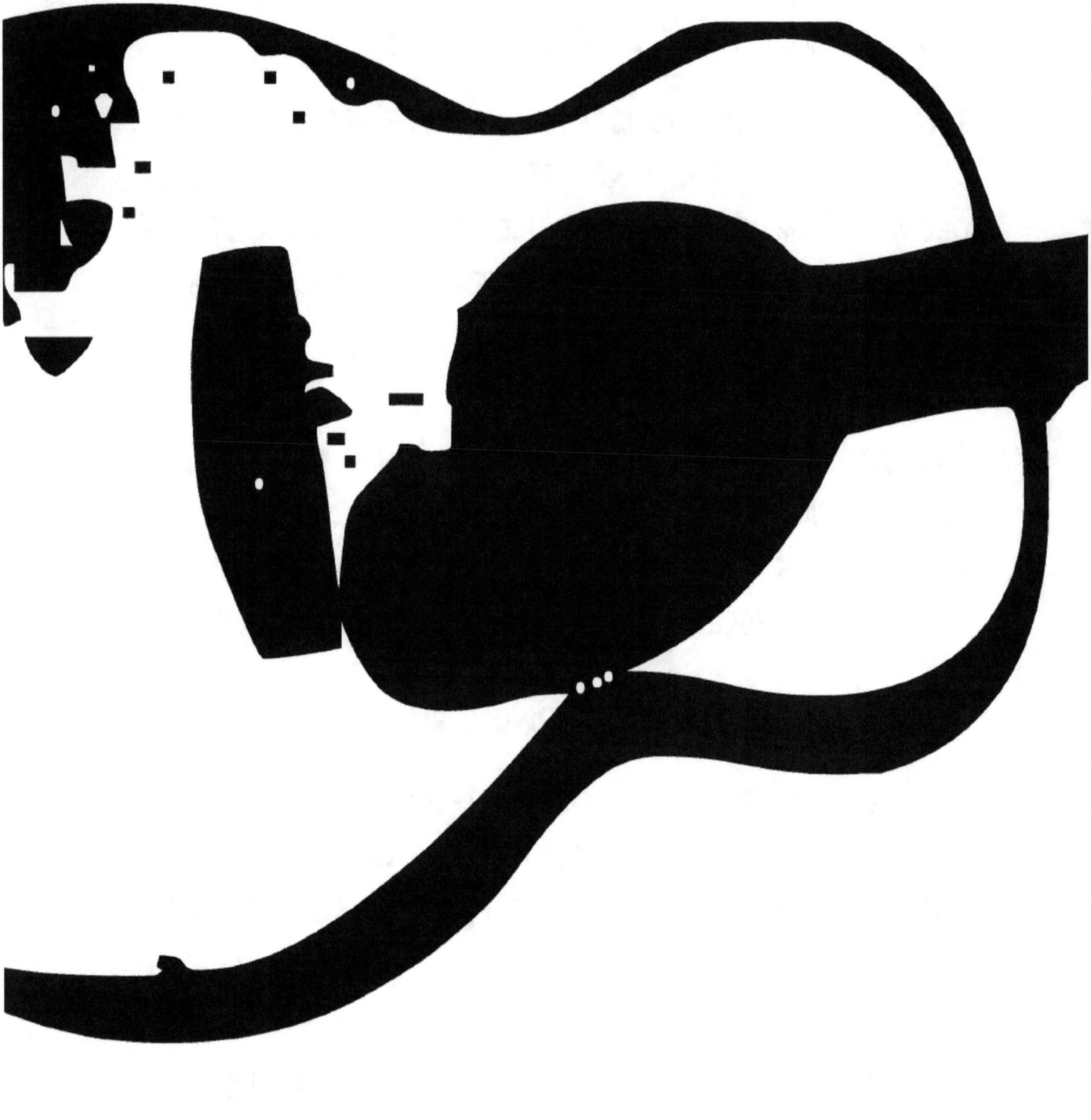

# TENTH POSITION

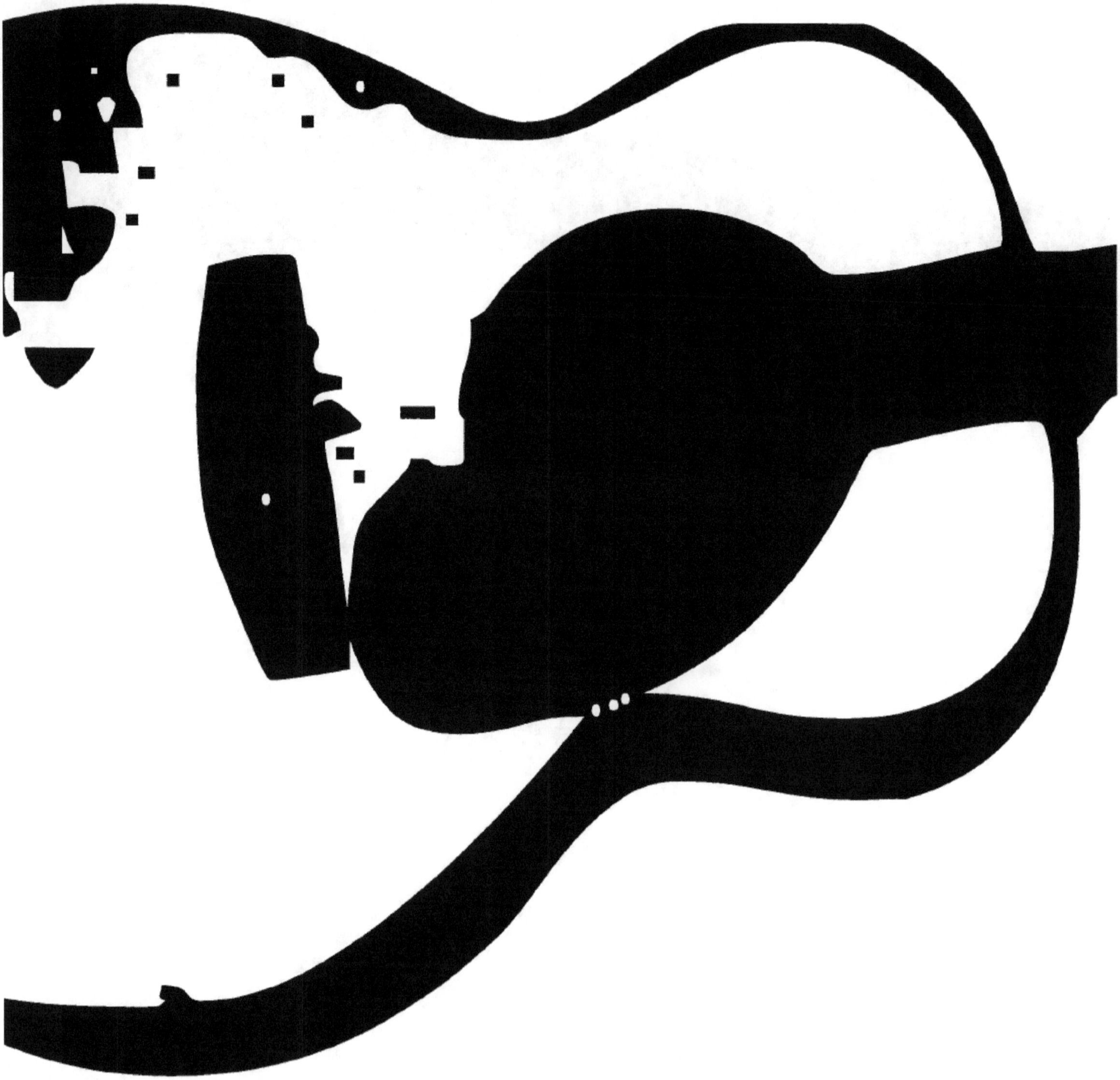

# THE C CHORDS AND SCALES

OR

"THE ②ND / ④TH STRING(S), 1ST & 4TH FINGER(S) SHAPES"

Fret
*10*

(Second String)

(Fourth String)

1 2 3 4

Fingers

THIS SHAPE CONSTRUCT UNDERSCORES ALL THE C CHORDS AND SCALES FOUND IN THE TENTH POSITION. THE MAIN C ROOT NOTE(S) ARE ON THE SECOND / FOURTH STRING(S), AND OBSERVE THE FIRST AND FOURTH FINGER(S) DO THE FRETTING. AN UNEXPECTED COROLLARY, AS THESE FINGERS BESTOW A FRESH SENSE OF TECHNICAL FEEL TO THE FRETTING HAND IN THAT THE MAIN ROOT NOTE(S) FALL OUTSIDE THE TYPICAL SECOND AND THIRD FINGER REALM. THE "DOT(S)" GROUND THE FINGER WORK INVOLVED. ☞

# SOME OF THE C CHORD VOICINGS ASSOCIATED WITH THE GUITAR'S TENTH POSITION ARE:

# SOME OF THE C SCALE VOICINGS ASSOCIATED WITH THE GUITAR'S TENTH POSITION ARE:

# FURTHER COMMENTARY...

AS EVIDENCED IN THE GRIDS ON THE PREVIOUS PAGE,
ALL C CHORDS AND SCALES COMPLEMENT THE TENTH
POSITION QUITE WELL, PLUS EACH ENSUING FORM AND
PATTERN CAN BE DUPLICATED IN ANY OTHER POSITION
TOO, WITH SLIGHT ADJUSTMENTS IN FINGERING. THE
**MAIN** C ROOT NOTE(S) ARE OBVIOUSLY FRETTED WITH
THE FIRST AND OR FOURTH FINGER(S) SEPARATELY OR
TOGETHER. BUT UNDERSTAND, WHEN DOING SO HERE
THE FIRST FINGER WILL FUNCTION LIKE A CAPO, AS IT
IS COMMON FOR IT TO BARRE A FEW NEARBY STRINGS.
IN CONTRAST, THE FOURTH FINGER REGULARLY SLURS
TO, HAMMERS ON OR PULLS OFF TO, ANY NOTES THAT
IT CAN WHEN IT CAN. ALSO, UNDERSTAND THAT THE
**MAIN** C ROOT NOTE(S) BEING AN OCTAVE AWAY FROM
EACH OTHER IS A GOOD SITUATION FOR THE FRETTING
HAND TO FIND ITSELF, AS IT'S POISED IN THE MIDDLE

OF THE PERFECT OCTAVE. THEN, WHEN A STRETCH IS NEEDED, THE FIRST AND OR FOURTH FINGER(S) OFTEN DEPENDABLY FRET THE NOTE, AS PICKING TECHNIQUES APPEAR A BIT MORE INTUITIVELY UNDERSTOOD IN THIS CONSTRUCT. LAST, REMEMBER TO UTILIZE THE OPEN STRINGS, SPECIFICALLY THE OPEN FIRST E STRING OR THE OPEN THIRD G POSSIBLY, AS THEY OCCASIONALLY ARE USED. ONCE INCORPORATED, OPEN STRINGS CAN ENHANCE THE SONOROUS QUALITIES OF THE MATERIAL, AND EXPAND FINGERING PROSPECTS.

EITHER **MAIN** C ROOT NOTE(S) ARE EQUAL, MUSICALLY SPEAKING, THE SAME IN TERMS OF MUSICAL PURPOSE. BUT DO NOT VOICE BOTH EVERY TIME, ALL THE TIME, IN EVERY C CHORD OR SCALE PLAYED.

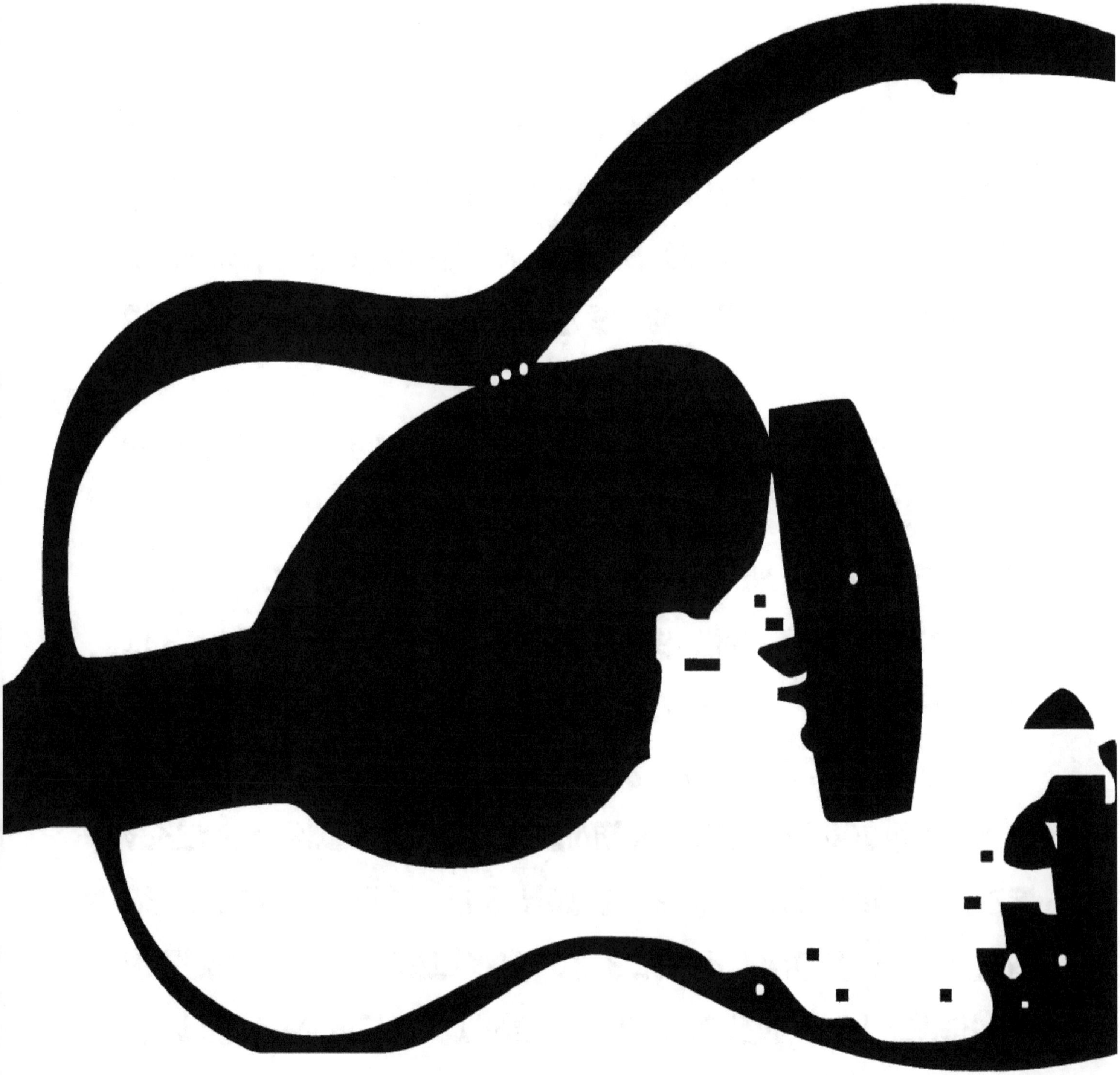

# The A Chords and Scales

## or
## "The ⑤TH String, 3RD Finger Shapes"

Fret
*10*

(Fifth String)

A

A

A

5

1  2  **3**  -4

Fingers

THE SUAVE "FIFTH STRING, THIRD FINGER" SHAPE CONSTRUCT UNDERSCORES ALL A CHORDS AND SCALES IN THE TENTH POSITION. THE **MAIN** A ROOT NOTE IS LOCATED ON THE FIFTH STRING, UNDER THE THIRD FINGER, THE THIRD FINGER FRETTING. THE "DOT" GROUNDS THE A FINGER WORK INVOLVED. ALSO NOTICE THE INDEX FINGER UNAVOIDABLY FRETS IT'S A ON THE FIRST STRING, FOR APPARENT REASONS. BUT THE PINKY MUST EITHER STRETCH, OR SLIDE, TO IT'S OWN ON THE THIRD. ☞

# SOME OF THE A CHORD VOICINGS ASSOCIATED WITH THE GUITAR'S TENTH POSITION ARE:

Augmented    Major    Minor    Diminished

1 2 3 4    1 2 3 4    1 2 3 4    1 2 3 4

1 2 3 4    1 2 3 4    1 2 3 4    1 2 3 4

# SOME OF THE A SCALE VOICINGS ASSOCIATED WITH THE GUITAR'S TENTH POSITION ARE:

Melodic Descending    Harmonic    Melodic Ascending    Major

1 2 3 4    1 2 3 4    1 2 3 4    1 2 3 4

1 2 3 4    1 2 3 4    1 2 3 4    1 2 3 4

13

# Further Commentary...

All tenth position A chords and scales here fit together in the position akin to crafted puzzle pieces, and any subsequent forms and patterns from here will work well in any other position also, notwithstanding the customary fingering tweak. The third and first fingers on the hand compliment each other best when playing this A material, those same fingers qualifying as well when moving the forms and patterns about the neck. Also, pay attention to the open strings, specifically the open fifth A and or either open E, they being readily found in the musical fold keeping things pleasingly desirable. That aside, look to the pair of A's one perfect octave away from the **main** A root note. They are in unison, and both are higher in pitch. And looking there,

OBVIOUSLY, THE A ON THE SECOND STRING IS PAIRED WITH THE **MAIN** A ROOT NOTE BY DESIGN, THE INDEX FINGER FRETTING. CONCERNING THE A ON THE THIRD STRING, IT REQUIRES A PINKY FINGER STRETCH. BUT GUITARISTS WILL SOMETIMES SLIDE THE PINKY THERE TO COUNTER ANYTHING TECHNICALLY AWKWARD.

KEEP IN MIND ALL A'S DISCUSSED IN THIS TEXT ARE MUSICALLY EQUAL. BUT THERE IS NO MUSICAL NEED TO VOICE ALL OF THEM EVERY TIME, NOR ALL AT THE SAME TIME, IN EVERY A CHORD OR SCALE PLAYED.

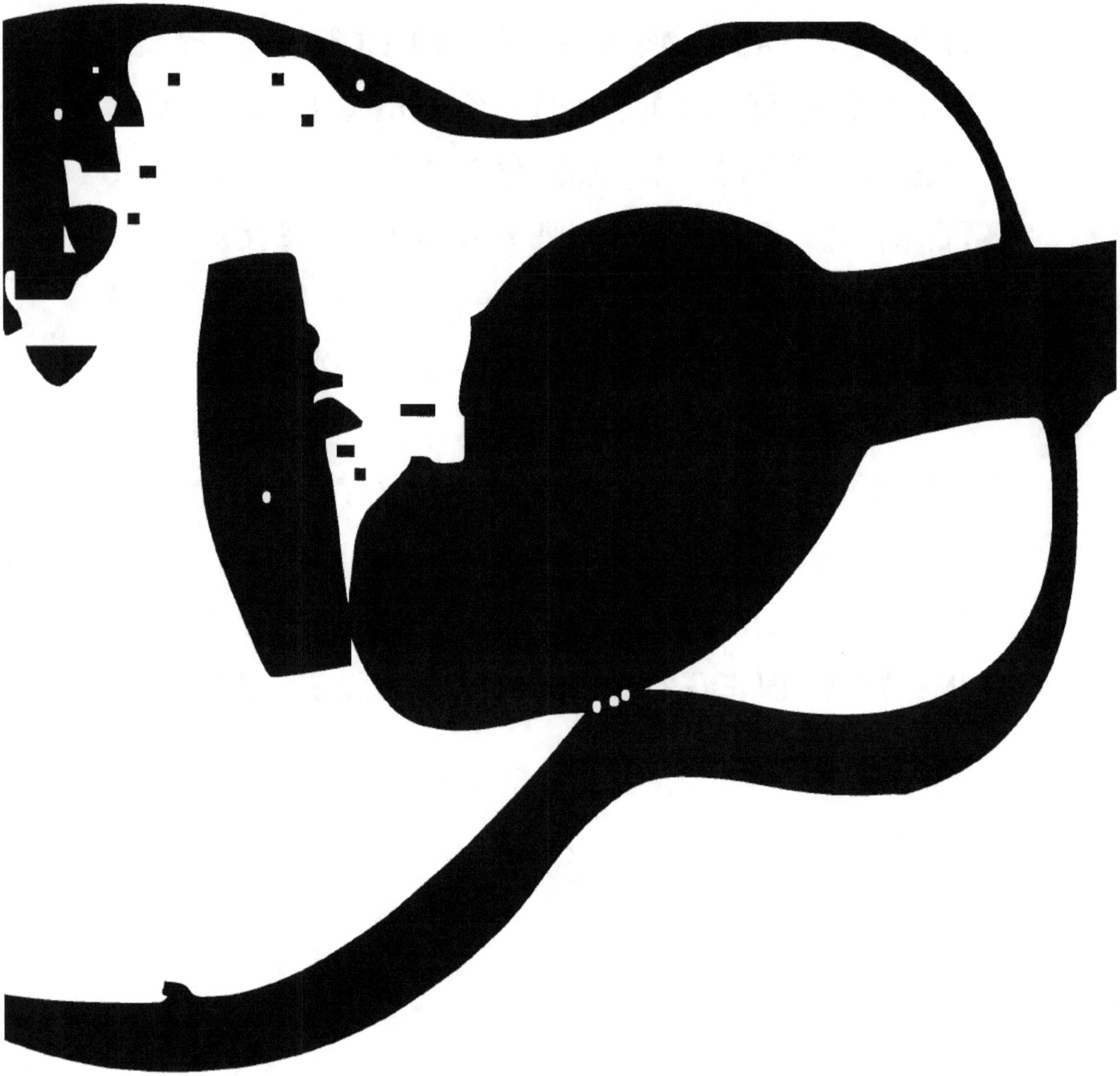

# THE G CHORDS AND SCALES

## OR
### "THE ③RD STRING, 3RD FINGER SHAPES"

Fret
*10*

(Third String)

G

G

1 2 **3** 4

Fingers

③

THIS UBIQUITOUS "THIRD STRING THIRD FINGER" SHAPE CONSTRUCT UNDERSCORES ALL THE G CHORDS AND SCALES IN THE TENTH POSITION. OBSERVE, THE ALL IMPORTANT **MAIN** G ROOT NOTE IS FIXED ON THE THIRD STRING, UNDERNEATH THE THIRD FINGER, WITH THAT FINGER FRETTING. THE BIG "DOT" HELPS GROUND THE G FINGER WORK INVOLVED. THAT SAID, THE REMAINING LOWER OCTAVE G ON THE FIFTH STRING OBLIGATES THE INDEX FINGER, COMFORTABLY, AS NO STRETCH IS REQUIRED. ☞

# SOME OF THE G CHORD VOICINGS ASSOCIATED WITH THE GUITAR'S TENTH POSITION ARE:

Augmented   Major   Minor   Diminished

1 2 3 4   1 2 3 4   1 2 3 4   1 2 3 4

1 2 3 4   1 2 3 4   1 2 3 4   1 2 3 4

# SOME OF THE G SCALE VOICINGS ASSOCIATED WITH THE GUITAR'S TENTH POSITION ARE:

Melodic Descending   Harmonic   Melodic Ascending   Major

1 2 3 4   1 2 3 4   1 2 3 4   1 2 3 4

1 2 3 4   1 2 3 4   1 2 3 4   1 2 3 4

19

# FURTHER COMMENTARY...

CURIOUS HOW ALL G CHORDS AND SCALES FIT IN THE
TENTH POSITION FRAMEWORK SO NEATLY AS THEY DO,
AND KNOW THAT ALL ENSUING FORMS AND PATTERNS
FUNCTION SUPERBLY IN THE POSITIONS THAT REMAIN,
MIND THE SUBTLE FINGERING ADJUSTMENTS, IF ANY.
AS EVIDENCED IN THE GRIDS ON THE PREVIOUS PAGE,
THE THIRD AND FIRST FINGERS WORK TOGETHER BEST
WHEN PLAYING THIS G MATERIAL, AND NOTICE THE G
ON THE FIFTH STRING IS PAIRED OVER AND OVER WITH
THE **MAIN** G ROOT NOTE IN QUESTION.  ALSO OBSERVE
THE OPEN THIRD G STRING, AS IT'S OFTEN INCLUDED
IN THE G FINGER WORK FOR ITS SONOROUS QUALITIES.
IT'S IMPORTANT TO POINT OUT THAT THE SAME THIRD
G STRING IS ONE OCTAVE BENEATH THE **MAIN** G ROOT
NOTE, AND IT'S IN UNISON WITH THE G ON THE FIFTH
STRING, FODDER FOR MUSICAL EXPLORATION.

In the tenth position, there're certain fingering issues that can potentially arise involving the third or ring finger, particularly when fretting the G major chord. Look, as seen in the grids, the finger may either barre some three strings involved in the major chord, or it stays put as the respective middle and pinky fingers assist, even though the fret space is rather narrow in this instance. However, either way do consider that efficient fingering, the functional tension, is derived from voice leading requirements.

In terms of music, all G's are considered equal. However, don't voice all of them all the time in every single G chord or scale played.

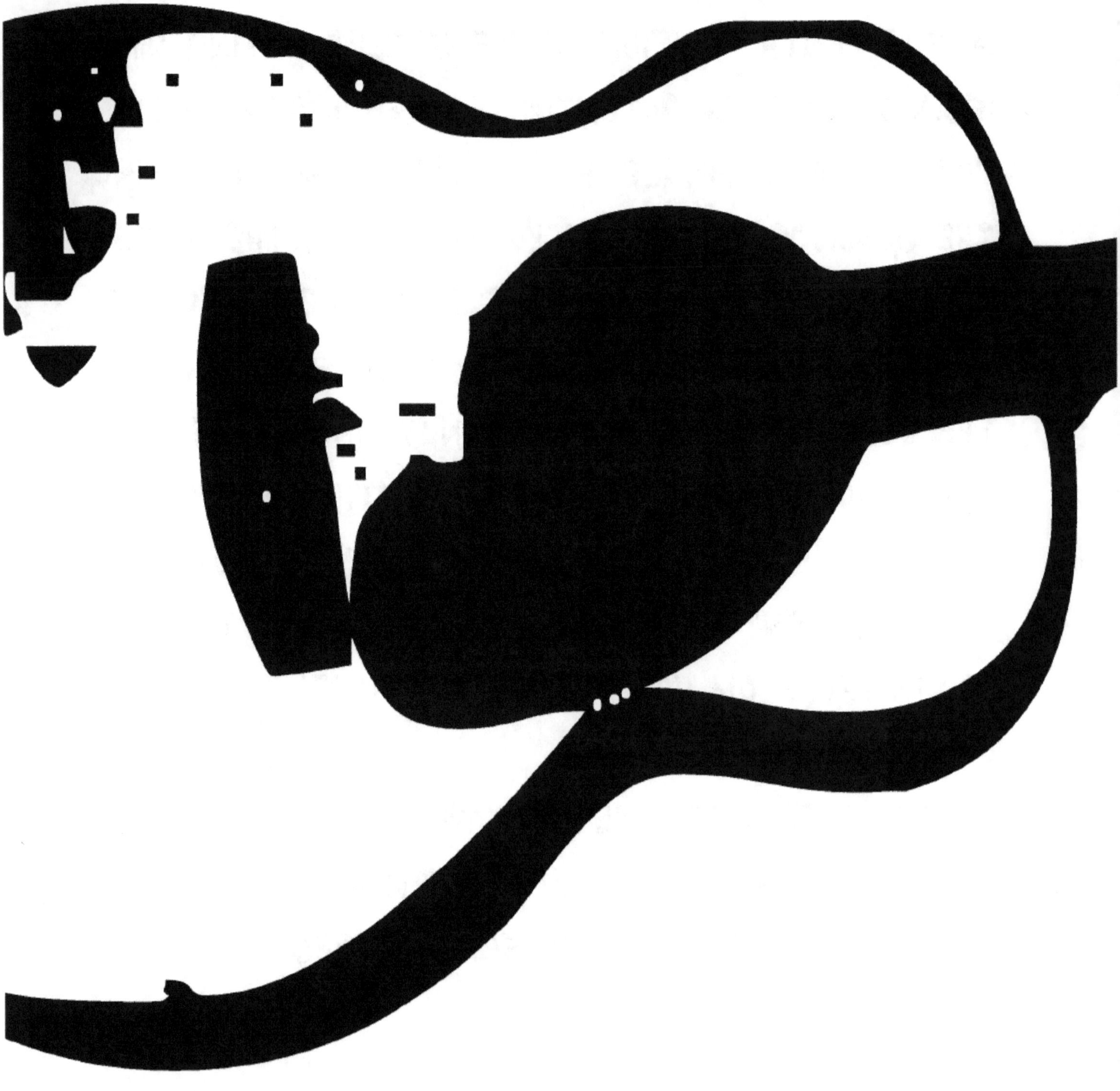

# THE E CHORDS AND SCALES

OR

## "THE ①ˢᵀ / ⑥ᵀᴴ STRING(S), 3ᴿᴰ FINGER SHAPES"

Fret
*10*

(First String)　　　　E　　　　　　　　　　1

E

E

(Sixth String)　　　　E　　　　　　　　　　6

1-　　2 **3** -4

Fingers

**T**HIS "FIRST / SIXTH STRING(S) THIRD FINGER" SHAPE CONSTRUCT UNDERSCORES ALL THE E CHORDS AND SCALES IN THE TENTH POSITION. NOTICE THE **MAIN** E ROOT NOTE(S) ARE SITUATED ON THE FIRST / SIXTH STRING(S) VIA THE THIRD FINGER, THAT FINGER FRETTING. THE SUPPLEMENTARY E'S ON THE THIRD AND OR FOURTH STRINGS ARE ONE OCTAVE AWAY, AND IN UNISON. THE RELEVANT INDEX AND OR PINKY FINGER MUST STRETCH OR, IN ALL PROBABILITY, SLIDE TO VOICE THEM. ☞

# SOME OF THE E CHORD VOICINGS ASSOCIATED WITH THE GUITAR'S TENTH POSITION ARE:

Augmented    Major    Minor    Diminished

1 2 3 4   1 2 3 4   1 2 3 4   1 2 3 4

1 2 3 4   1 2 3 4   1 2 3 4   1 2 3 4

# SOME OF THE E SCALE VOICINGS ASSOCIATED WITH THE GUITAR'S TENTH POSITION ARE:

Melodic Descending    Harmonic    Melodic Ascending    Major

1 2 3 4   1 2 3 4   1 2 3 4   1 2 3 4

1 2 3 4   1 2 3 4   1 2 3 4   1 2 3 4

# FURTHER COMMENTARY...

ALL THE E CHORDS AND SCALES FOUND IN THE GRIDS FROM THE PREVIOUS PAGE FIT TOGETHER LIKE PUZZLE PIECES, AND THEIR SUBSEQUENT FORMS OR PATTERNS CAN BE DUPLICATED ELSEWHERE ALONG THE NECK AS WELL. OBSERVE THE THIRD AND FIRST FINGERS WORK BEST NAVIGATING THE E MATERIAL, THE THIRD FINGER FRETTING THE **MAIN** E ROOT NOTE(S) SEPARATELY OR, WITH THE HELP OF THE PINKY, TOGETHER. BUT KNOW THE THIRD FINGER MAINTAINS ITS PRECEDENCE IN THE FINGER WORK, THIS AS EITHER **MAIN** E ROOT NOTE(S) FALL UNDER IT. THAT SAID, IT'S VERY IMPORTANT TO UNDERSTAND THE INDEX FINGER WILL BE STRETCHING AND BARRING A GOOD DEAL OF THE TIME. OTHERWISE TO PUT IT HONESTLY, ANY TENTH POSITION E CHORD OR SCALE INVOLVING THE THIRD STRING WILL REQUIRE THE INDEX FINGER TO STRETCH OR BARRE. THE SAME

DOES NOT READILY APPLY TO THE PINKY THOUGH, AS IT DOES NOT BARRE ALL THE TIME.  HOWEVER, THE E ON THE FOURTH STRING DOES NECESSITATE A FINGER STRETCH.  BUT QUITE OFTEN GUITARISTS WILL SLIDE THE PINKY TO AND FROM INSTEAD AND NOT STRETCH THE FINGER UNCOMFORTABLY.  LAST IT'S A PRACTICAL GIVEN THAT THE GUITAR'S OPEN STRINGS, ESPECIALLY THE OPEN E'S, WILL BE INCLUDED IN SOME OF THE E VOICINGS ON GUITAR.

ALL E'S DISCUSSED IN THIS BOOK ARE EQUIVALENT IN TERMS OF MUSICAL FUNCTION.  HOWEVER NOT ALL OF THEM NEED TO BE VOICED EACH AND EVERY TIME, OR ALL SIMULTANEOUSLY, IN THE E CHORDS AND SCALES PLAYED.

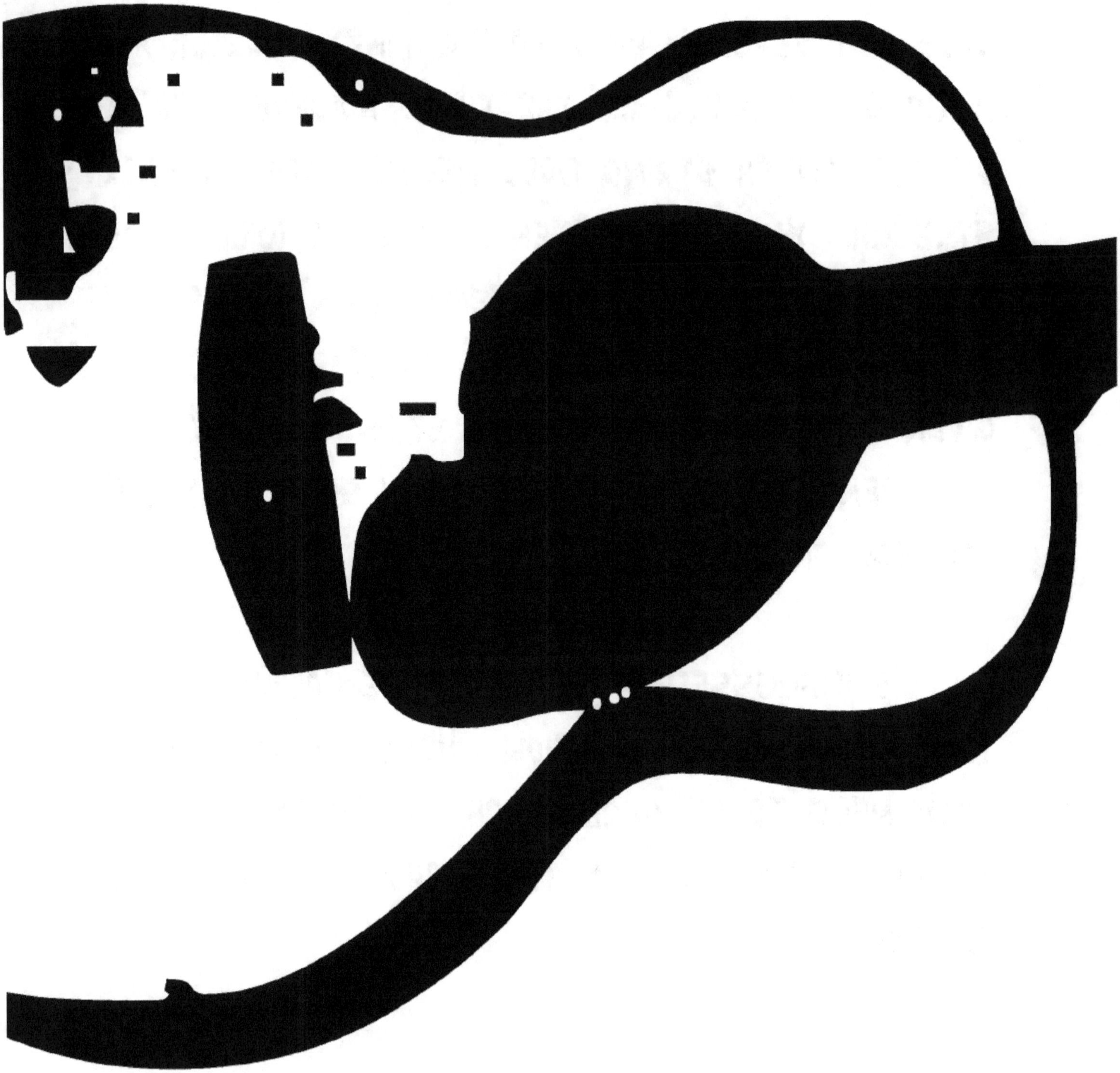

# THE D CHORDS AND SCALES

OR

"THE ④TH STRING, 3RD FINGER SHAPES"

29

Fret
*10*

**D**

(Fourth String)

**D** ④

**D**

**1 2 3 4**

Fingers

THIS RENOWNED "FOURTH STRING THIRD FINGER" SHAPE CONSTRUCT UNDERSCORES ALL THE D CHORDS AND SCALES IN THE TENTH POSITION. THE <u>MAIN</u> D ROOT NOTE IS SITUATED ON THE FOURTH STRING UNDERNEATH THE THIRD FINGER, THAT FINGER FRETTING. THE "DOT" GROUNDS THE D FINGER WORK INVOLVED. NOTICE THE FIRST OR SIXTH STRING D IS FRETTED WITH THE INDEX FINGER EITHER SEPARATELY OR BARRED. THAT ASIDE, THIS CONSTRUCT IS RATHER POPULAR AMONGST GUITAR PLAYERS. ☞

# SOME OF THE D CHORD VOICINGS ASSOCIATED WITH THE GUITAR'S TENTH POSITION ARE:

Augmented    Major    Minor    Diminished

# SOME OF THE D SCALE VOICINGS ASSOCIATED WITH THE GUITAR'S TENTH POSITION ARE:

Melodic Descending    Harmonic    Melodic Ascending    Major

# FURTHER COMMENTARY...

CLEVER HOW ALL THE D CHORDS AND SCALES MANAGE TO FIT INSIDE THE CONFINES OF THE TENTH POSITION FRAMEWORK. AND, WITH SOME VERY SLIGHT CHANGES TO THE FINGERING, ANY OF ITS ENSUING FORMS AND PATTERNS CAN BE LIFTED FROM HERE AND PLAYED IN ANY OTHER POSITION AS WELL. IN FACT, THESE VERY CHORDS AND SCALES HAVE OFTEN SERVED AS A BASIS TO THAT END, SO MUCH SO THAT THEIR SHAPES AND PATTERNS HAVE BECOME FAVORED IN THE LITERATURE. A GREAT EXAMPLE OF THIS IS THE MINOR PENTATONIC SCALE PATTERN, OR BLUES SCALE AS IT'S PORTRAYED IN THE GIVEN SCHOLARLY METHOD BOOKS AND VIDEOS TODAY. BUT IT DOES REMAIN PRUDENT TO MEMORIZE ALL THE D CHORDS AND SCALES PRESENTED HERE IN THE TENTH POSITION PRIOR TO THEN DUPLICATING ITS FORMS AND PATTERNS ELSEWHERE ABOUT THE NECK.

Notice the subtle way in which the third finger maintains its precedence throughout the tenth position D finger work, this mostly due to the MAIN D root note being fixed underneath it. It also helps, technically speaking, that there are no finger stretches between either one of the two octaves present, higher or lower. Finally, adding the open fourth D string, among others, to this material not only enhances the voicings here but also expands any fingering options.

All the D's discussed are identical in terms of musical purpose and function. However not all of them need to be voiced every time, or all at the same time, in every chord or scale played.

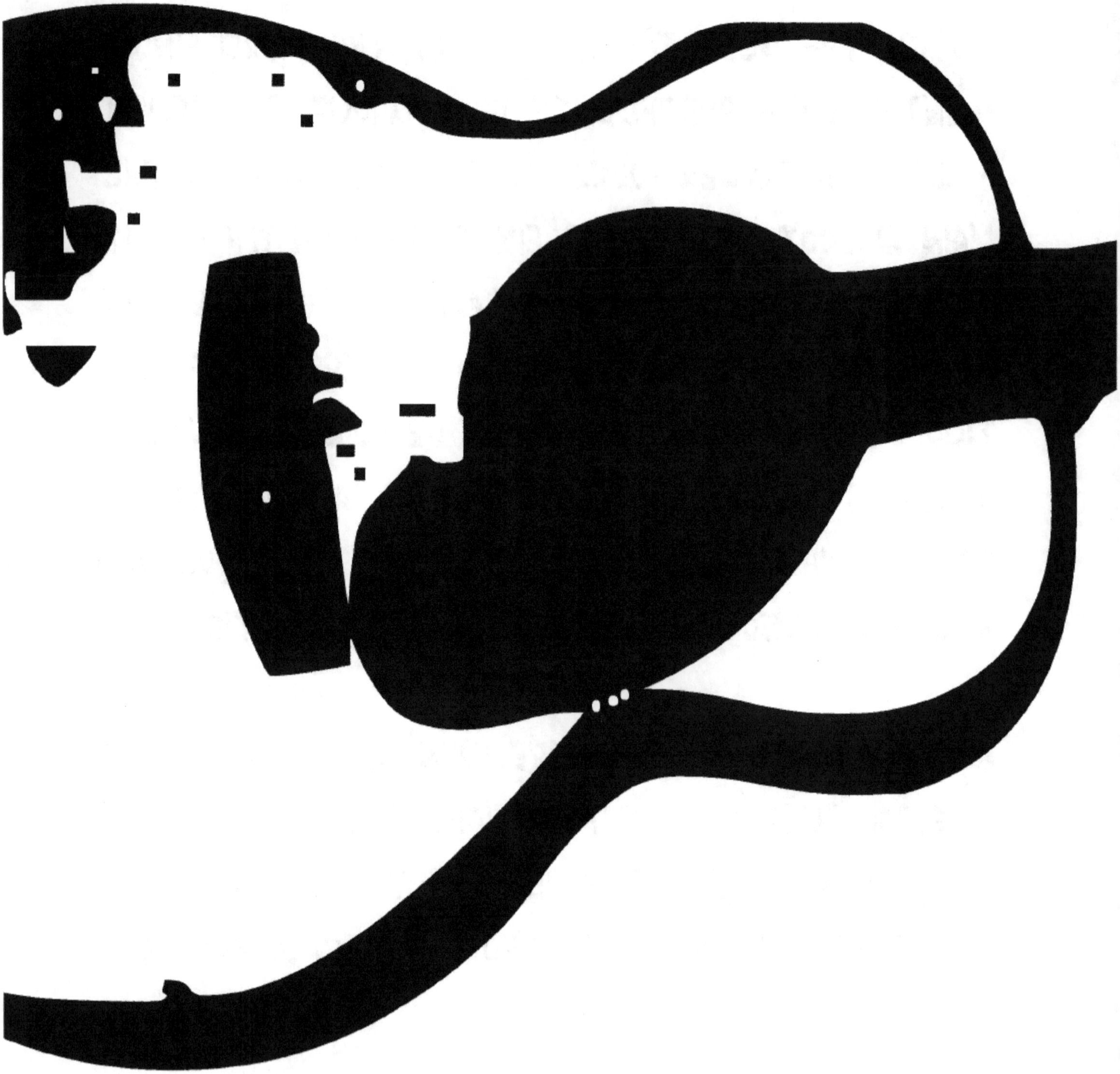

# ALPHABETICAL APPENDIX

35

Fret
*10*

(Fifth String)

A

A

Ⓐ

⑤

**1** **2** **3** **-4**

Fingers

# THE A CHORDS AND SCALES

## OR
## "THE ⑤ᵀᴴ STRING, 3ᴿᴰ FINGER SHAPES"

# ⑤TH, 3RD -A CHORDS

| Augmented | Major | Minor | Diminished |
|---|---|---|---|

1 2 3 4    1 2 3 4    1 2 3 4    1 2 3 4

Ⓢ

1 2 3 4    1 2 3 4    1 2 3 4    1 2 3 4

Ⓢ

# ⑤TH, 3RD -A SCALES

| Melodic Descending | Harmonic | Melodic Ascending | Major |
|---|---|---|---|

1 2 3 4    1 2 3 4    1 2 3 4    1 2 3 4

Ⓢ

1 2 3 4    1 2 3 4    1 2 3 4    1 2 3 4

Ⓢ

Fret
*10*

(Second String)

B

B

B

1-  2  **3**  -4

Fingers

# THE B CHORDS AND SCALES

## OR
## "THE ②ND STRING, 3RD FINGER SHAPES"

# ②ʳᵈ, 3ʳᵈ – B Chords

| Augmented | Major | Minor | Diminished |
|---|---|---|---|

1 2 3 4   1 2 3 4   1 2 3 4   1 2 3 4

1 2 3 4   1 2 3 4   1 2 3 4   1 2 3 4

# ②ʳᵈ, 3ʳᵈ – B Scales

| Melodic Descending | Harmonic | Melodic Ascending | Major |
|---|---|---|---|

1 2 3 4   1 2 3 4   1 2 3 4   1 2 3 4

1 2 3 4   1 2 3 4   1 2 3 4   1 2 3 4

38

Fret
*10*

(Second String)

(Fourth String)

**1** <sup></sup>2 3 **4**

Fingers

# THE C CHORDS AND SCALES

OR

"THE ②ND / ④TH STRING(S), 1ST & 4TH FINGER(S) SHAPES"

# ②ND ④TH, 1ST & 4TH – C CHORDS

| Augmented | Major | Minor | Diminished |
|---|---|---|---|

1 2 3 4    1 2 3 4    1 2 3 4    1 2 3 4

1 2 3 4    1 2 3 4    1 2 3 4    1 2 3 4

# ②ND ④TH, 1ST & 4TH – C SCALES

| Melodic Descending | Harmonic | Melodic Ascending | Major |
|---|---|---|---|

1 2 3 4    1 2 3 4    1 2 3 4    1 2 3 4

1 2 3 4    1 2 3 4    1 2 3 4    1 2 3 4

Fret
*10*

D

(Fourth String)                    D                                    ④

1  2  **3** 4

Fingers

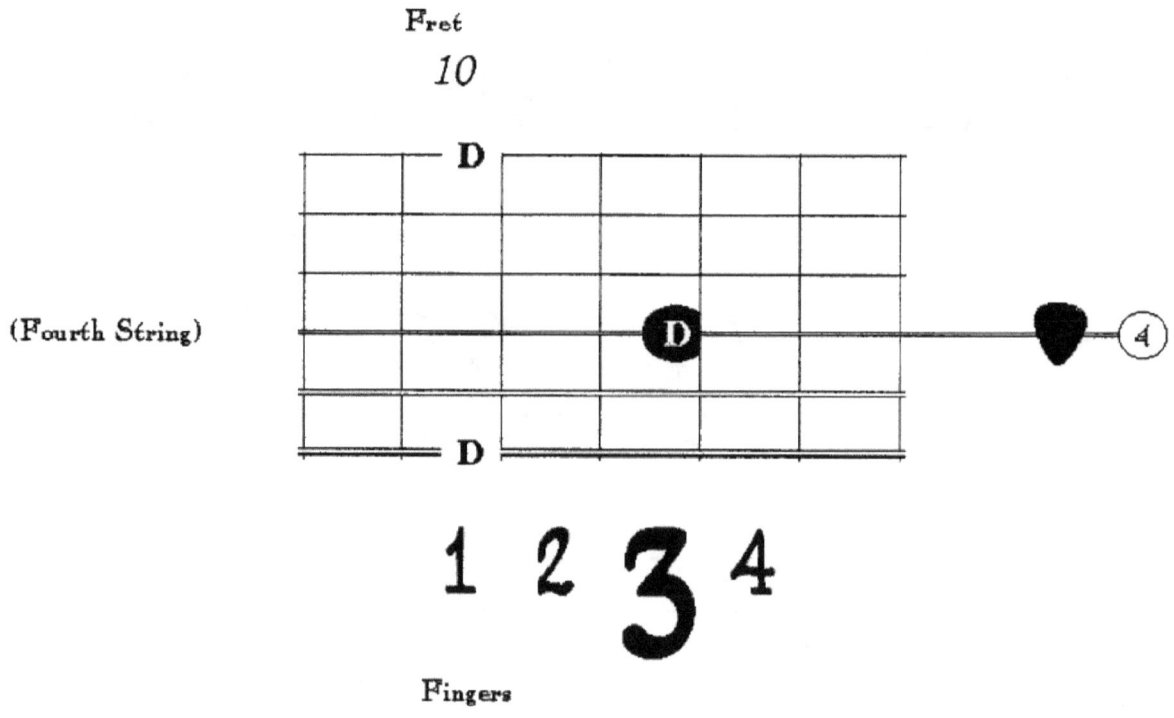

# THE D CHORDS AND SCALES

## OR
## "THE ④TH STRING, 3RD FINGER SHAPES"

# ④TH, 3RD -D CHORDS

# ④TH, 3RD -D SCALES

Fret

*10*

(First String)

(Sixth String)

E

E

E

E

1-    2 **3** -4

Fingers

# THE **E** CHORDS AND SCALES

## OR

### "THE ①ST / ⑥TH STRING(S), 3RD FINGER SHAPES"

# ①ˢᵗ ⑥ᵀᴴ, 3ᴿᴰ – E Chords

Augmented · Major · Minor · Diminished

# ①ˢᵗ ⑥ᵀᴴ, 3ᴿᴰ – E Scales

Melodic Descending · Harmonic · Melodic Ascending · Major

45

Fret

*10*

(First String)

(Third String)

(Sixth String)

1 2 3 4

Fingers

# THE F CHORDS AND SCALES

OR

"THE ①ST / ③RD / ⑥TH STRING(S), 1ST & 4TH FINGER(S) SHAPES"

# ①ST ③RD ⑥TH, 1ST & 4TH -F CHORDS

Augmented　　Major　　Minor　　Diminished

# ①ST ③RD ⑥TH, 1ST & 4TH -F SCALES

Melodic Descending　　Harmonic　　Melodic Ascending　　Major

Fret
*10*

(Third String)

G

G

1 2 3 4

Fingers

# THE G CHORDS AND SCALES

OR

"THE ③ʳᵈ STRING, 3ʳᵈ FINGER SHAPES"

48

# ③ᴿᴰ, 3ᴿᴰ – G CHORDS

| Augmented | Major | Minor | Diminished |
|---|---|---|---|

1 2 3 4   1 2 3 4   1 2 3 4   1 2 3 4

⑤

⑤

1 2 3 4   1 2 3 4   1 2 3 4   1 2 3 4

⑤

# ③ᴿᴰ, 3ᴿᴰ – G SCALES

| Melodic Descending | Harmonic | Melodic Ascending | Major |
|---|---|---|---|

1 2 3 4   1 2 3 4   1 2 3 4   1 2 3 4

⑤

1 2 3 4   1 2 3 4   1 2 3 4   1 2 3 4

⑤

49

Fret
*10*

A

A

(Fifth String)

Ⓐ

A

⑤

1 2 **3** -4

Fingers

# THE A CHORDS AND SCALES

## OR

## "THE ⑤TH STRING, 3RD FINGER SHAPES"

# ⑤<sup>TH</sup>, 3<sup>RD</sup> – A CHORDS

| Augmented | Major | Minor | Diminished |
|---|---|---|---|

1 2 3 4    1 2 3 4    1 2 3 4    1 2 3 4

1 2 3 4    1 2 3 4    1 2 3 4    1 2 3 4

# ⑤<sup>TH</sup>, 3<sup>RD</sup> – A SCALES

| Melodic Descending | Harmonic | Melodic Ascending | Major |
|---|---|---|---|

1 2 3 4    1 2 3 4    1 2 3 4    1 2 3 4

1 2 3 4    1 2 3 4    1 2 3 4    1 2 3 4

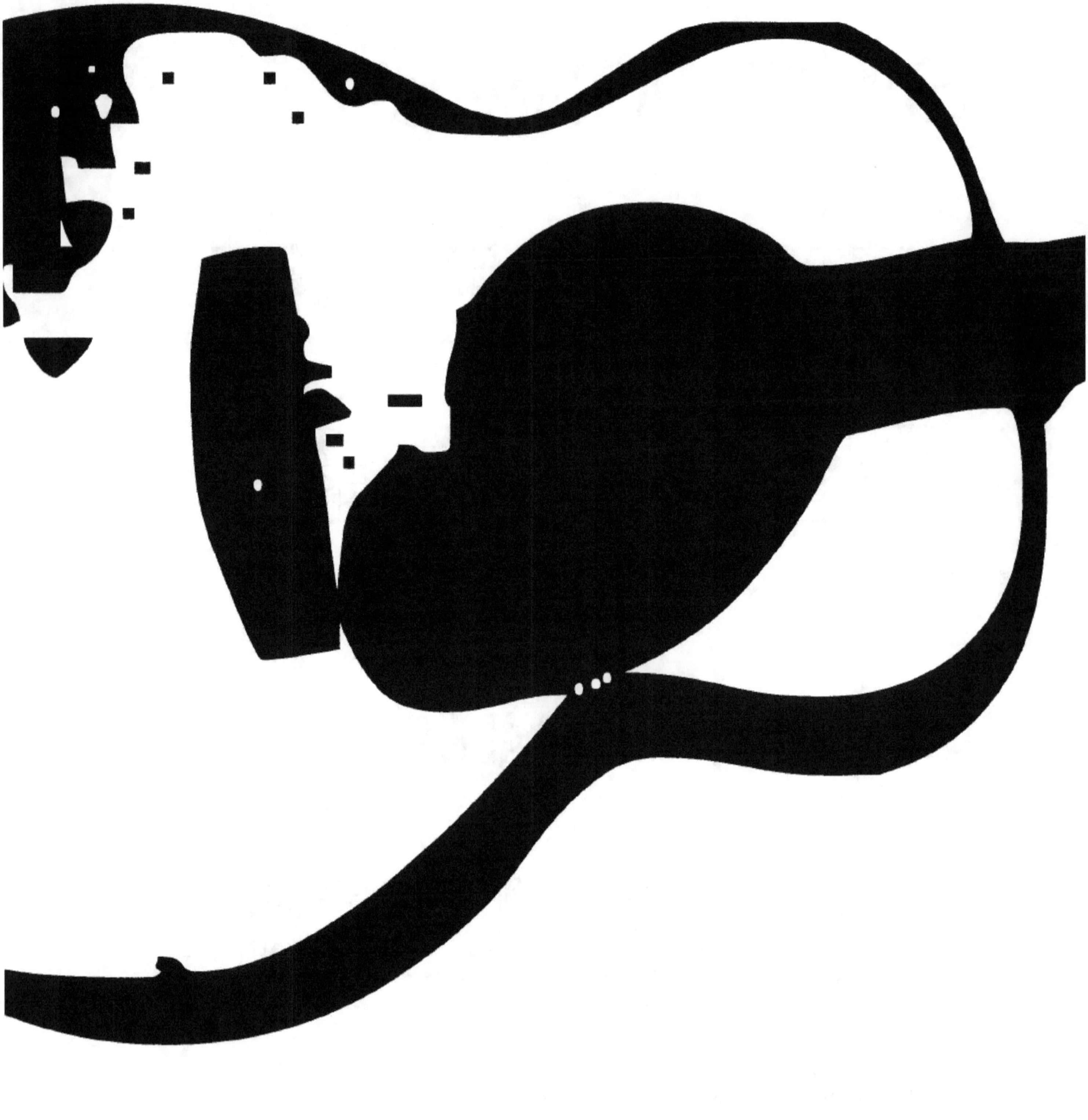

# Notation & Tablature

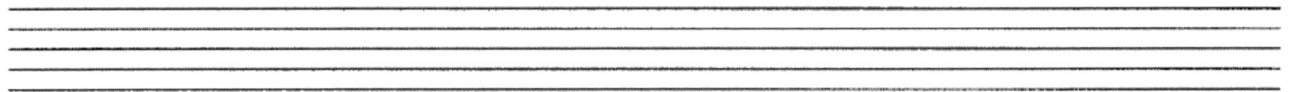

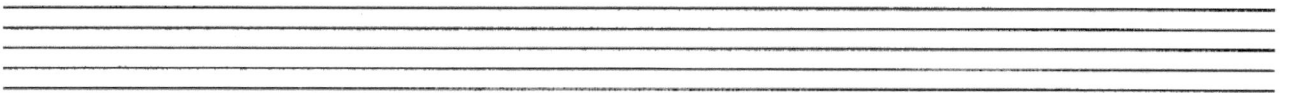

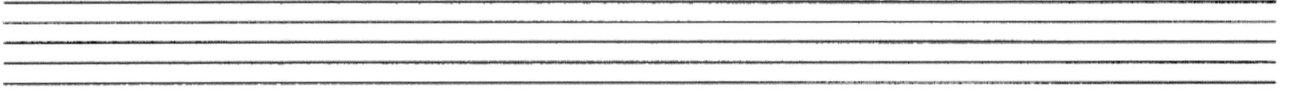

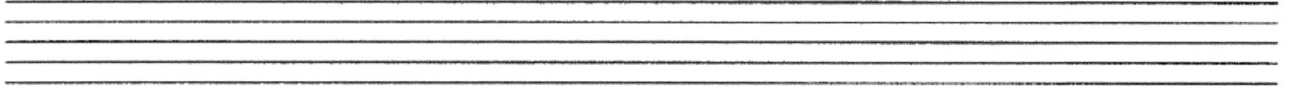

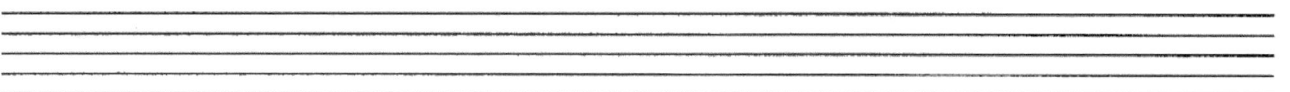

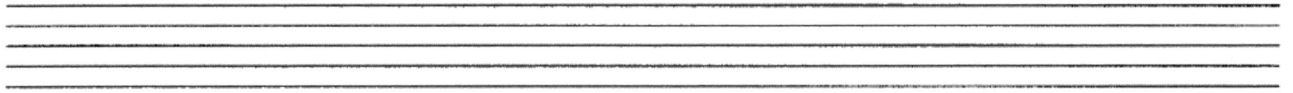

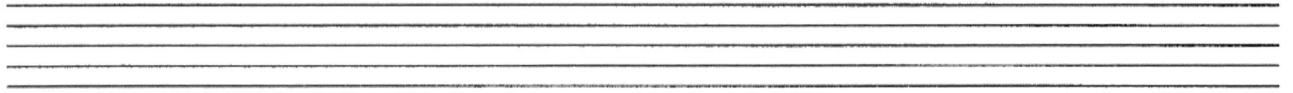

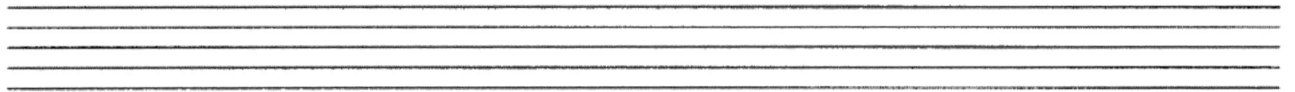

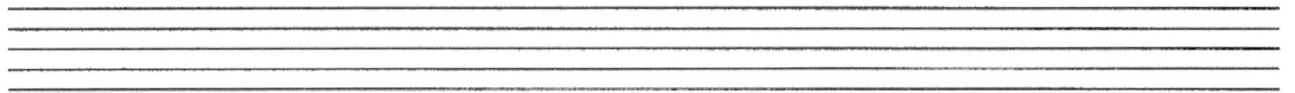

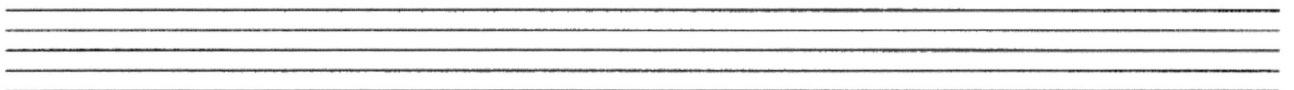

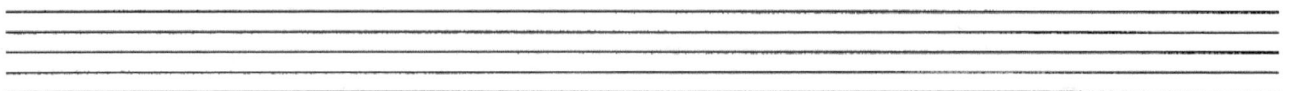

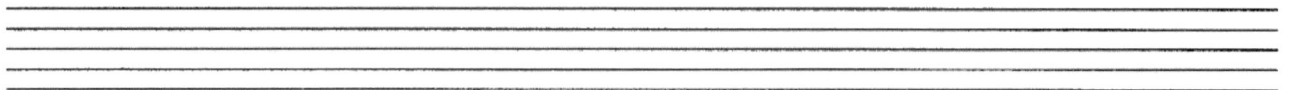

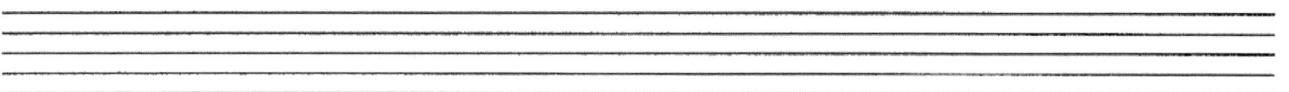

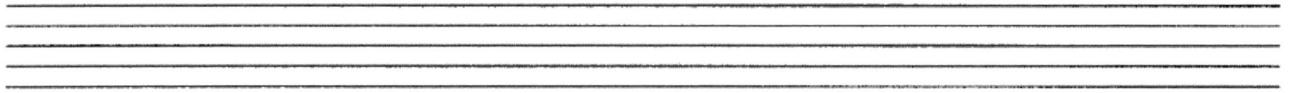

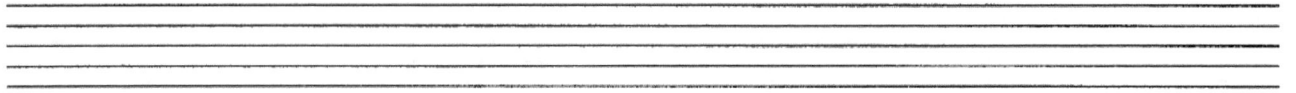

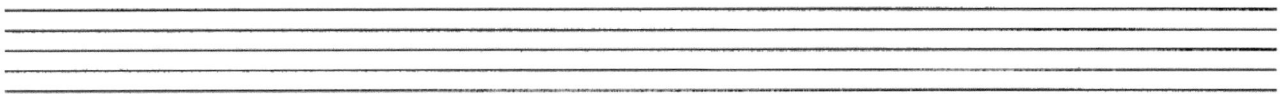

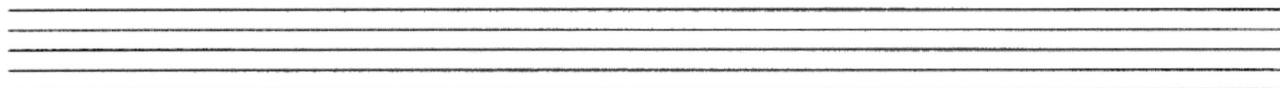

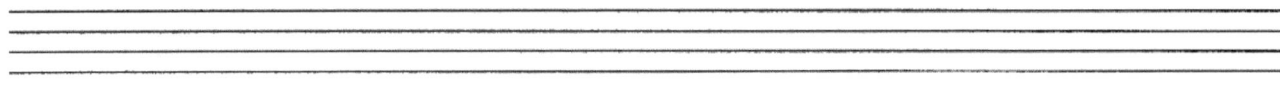

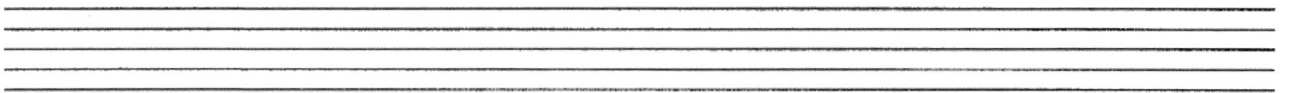

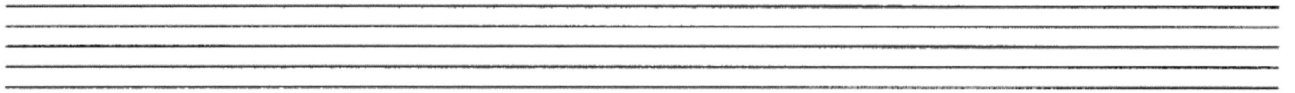

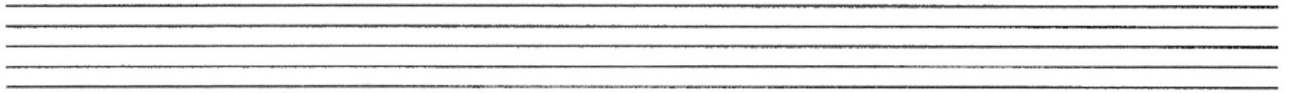

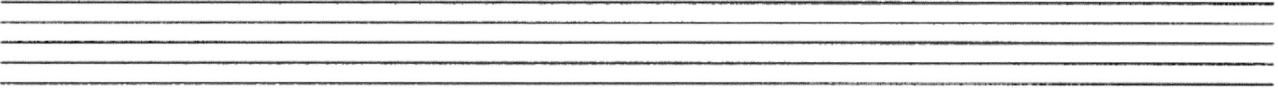

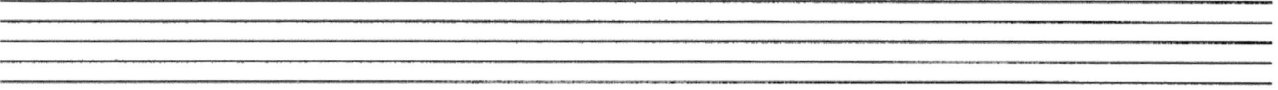

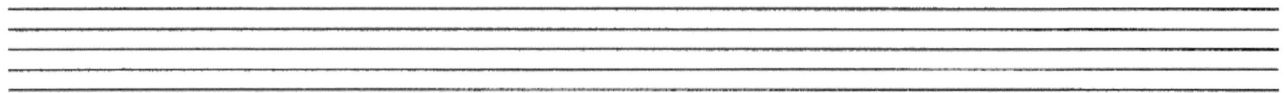

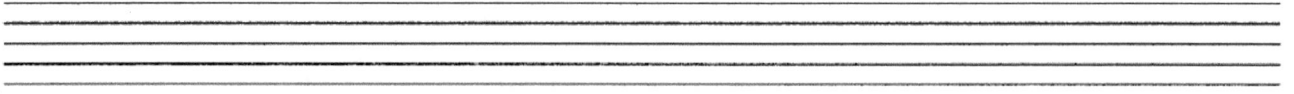

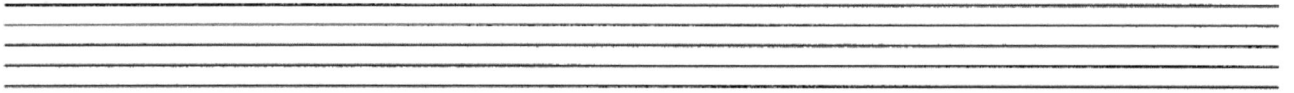

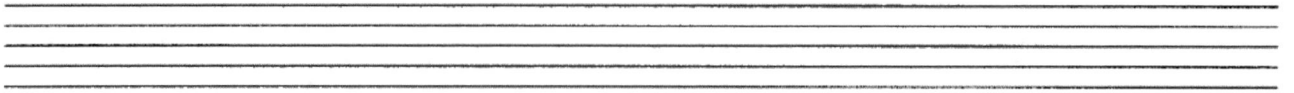

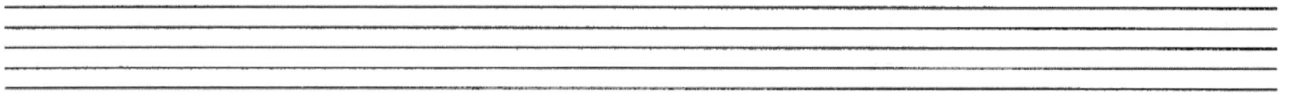

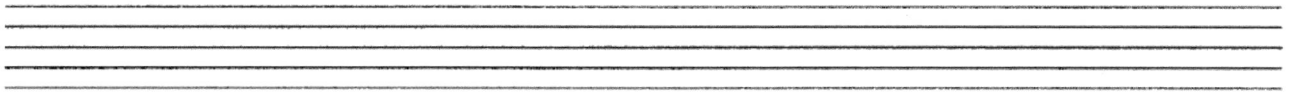

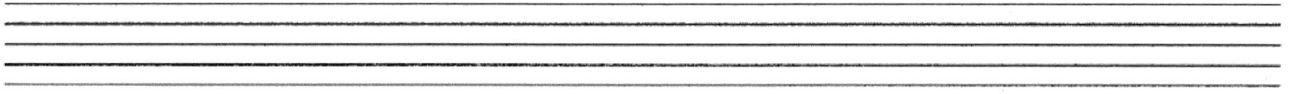

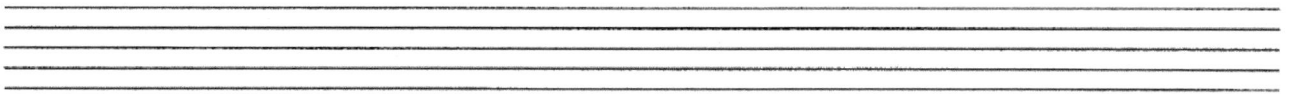

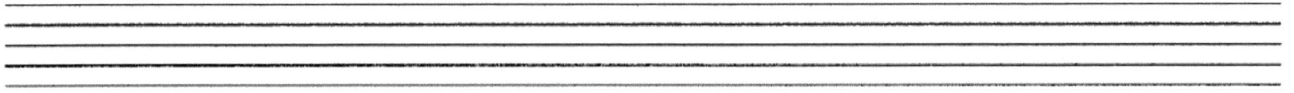

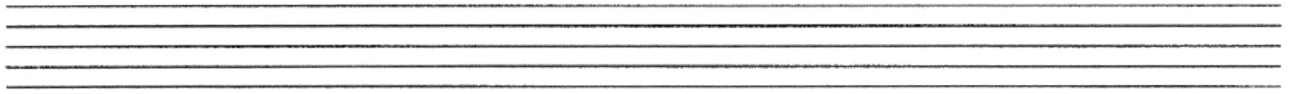

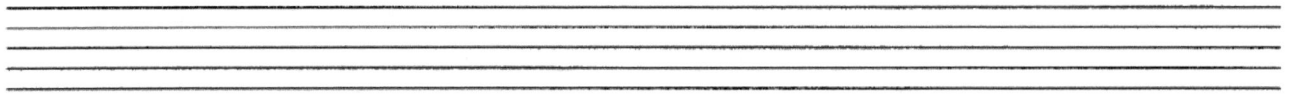

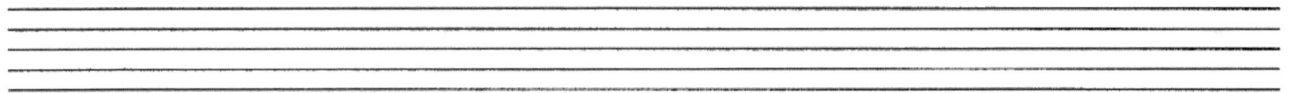

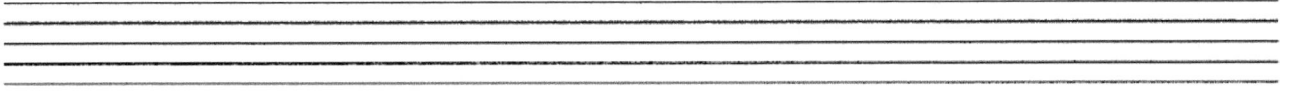

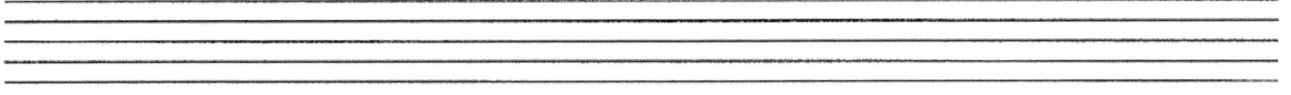

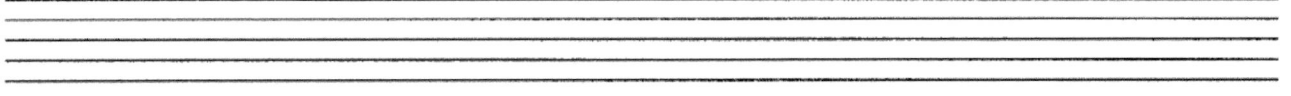

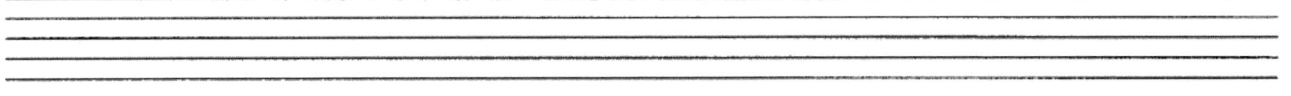

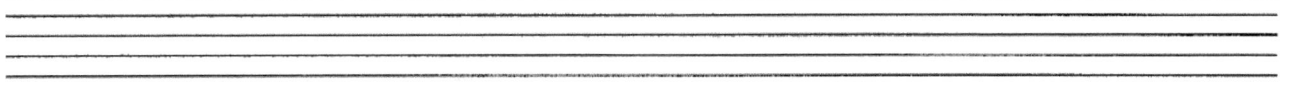

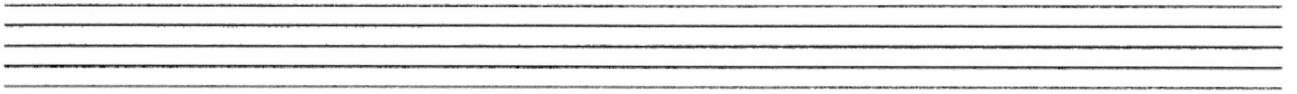

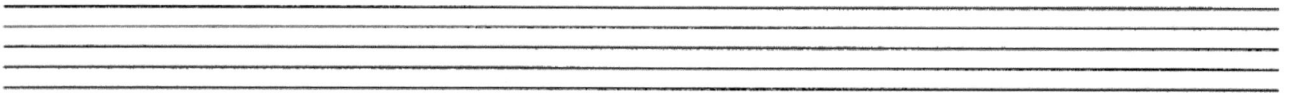

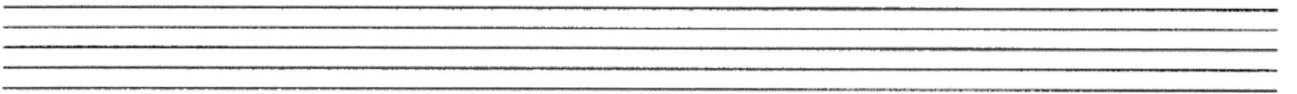

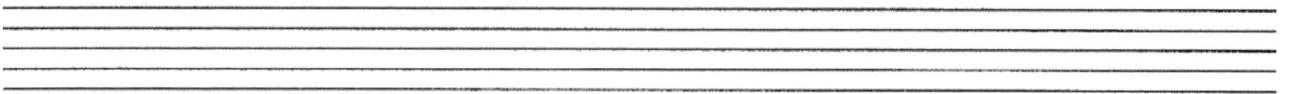

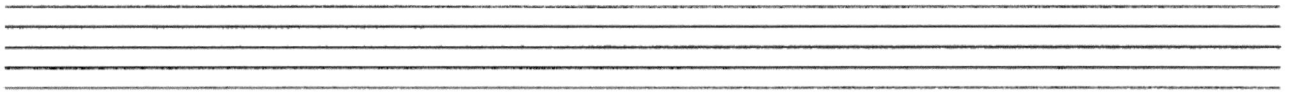

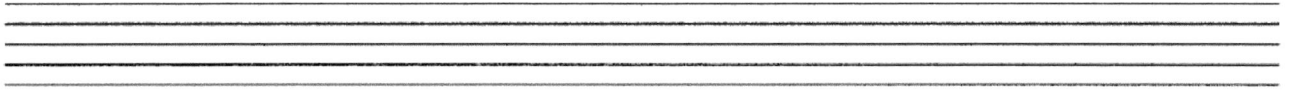

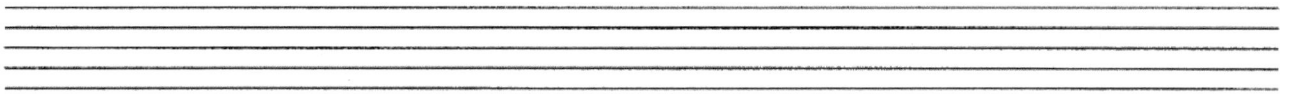

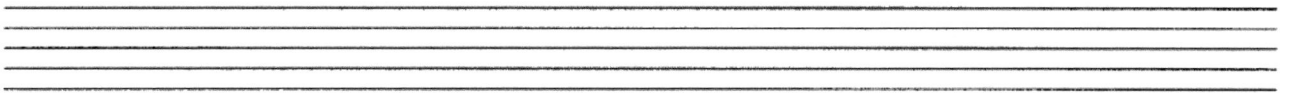

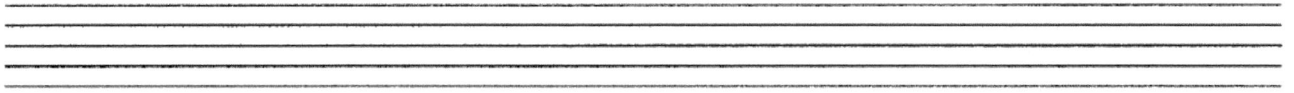

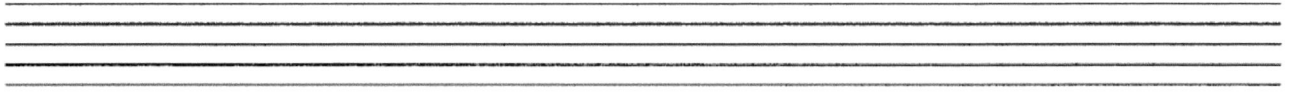

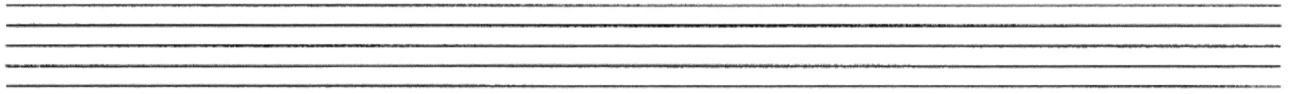

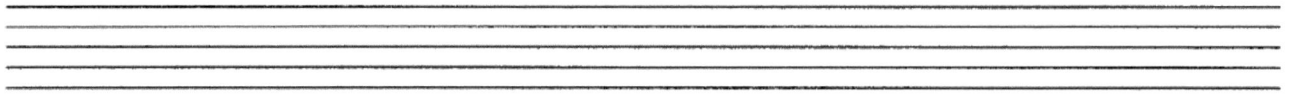

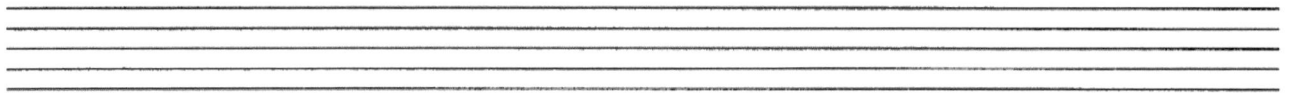

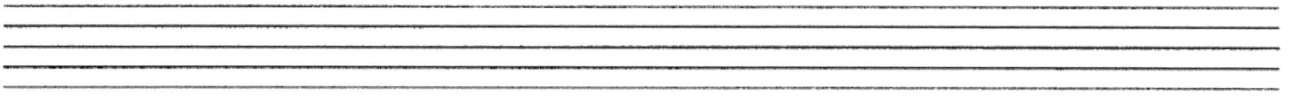

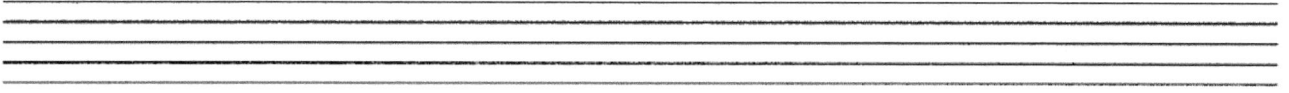

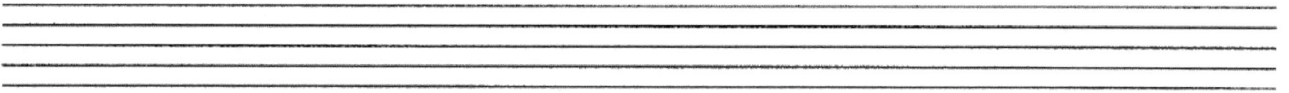

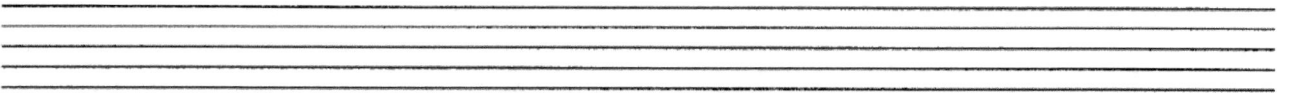

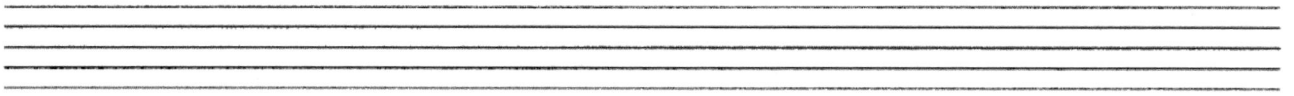

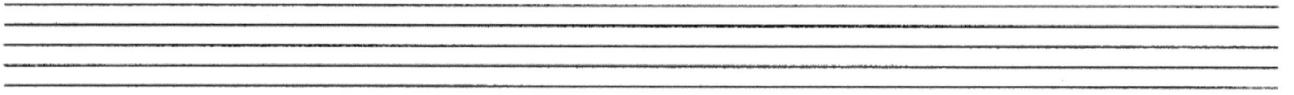

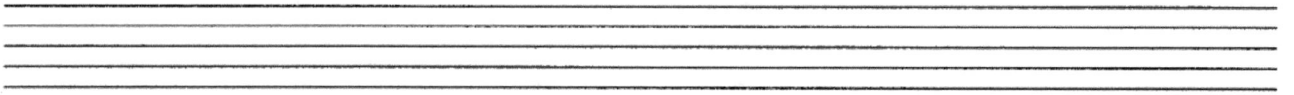

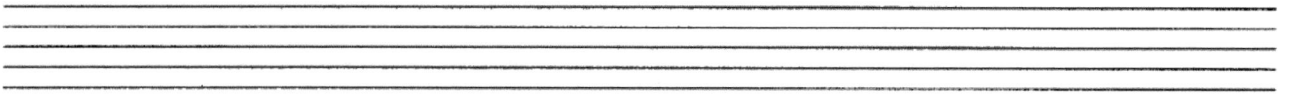

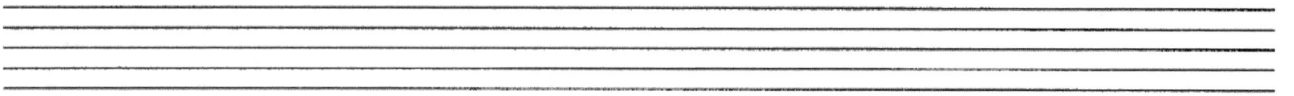

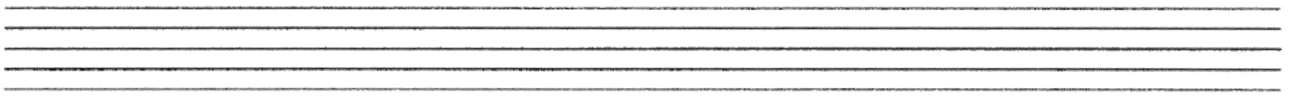

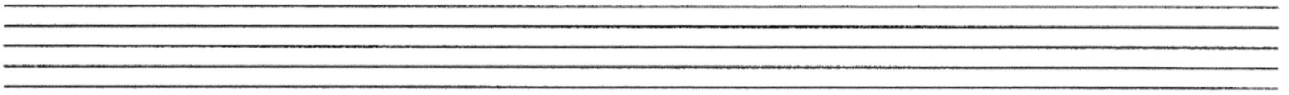

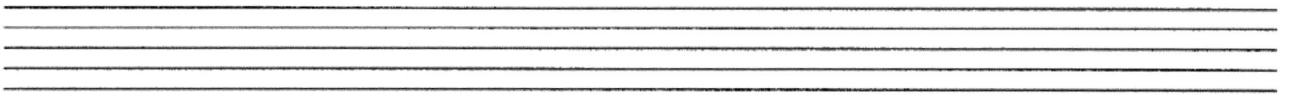

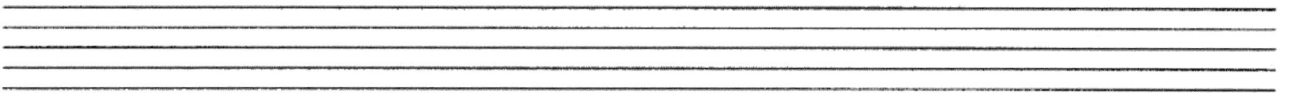

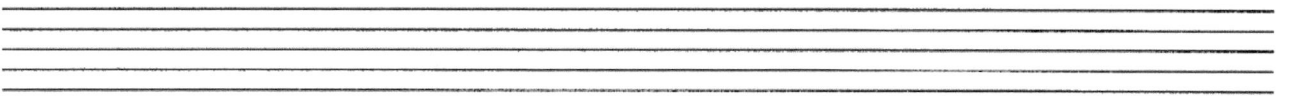

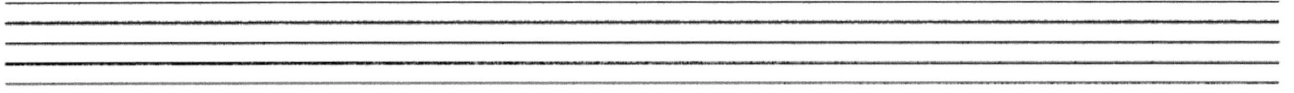

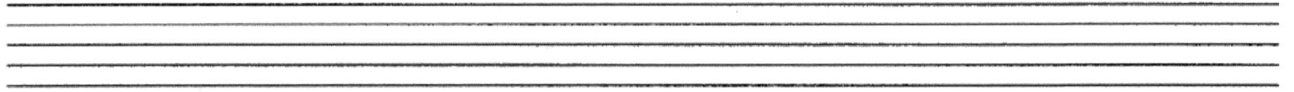

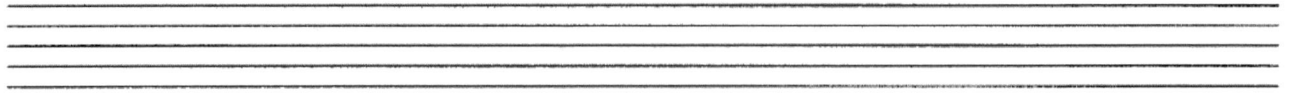

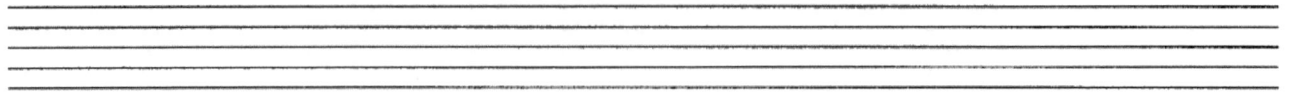

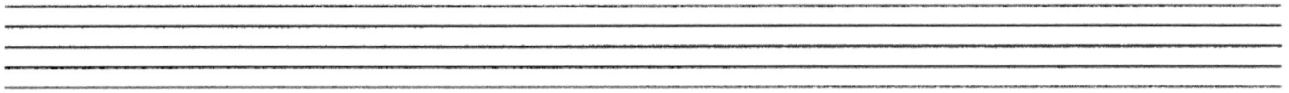

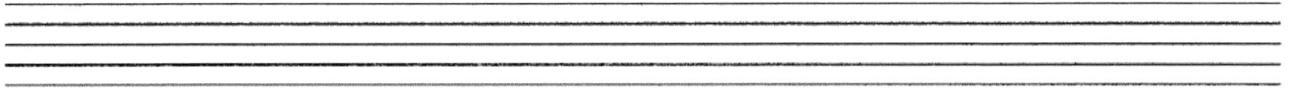

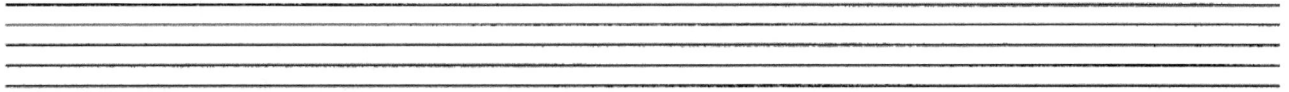

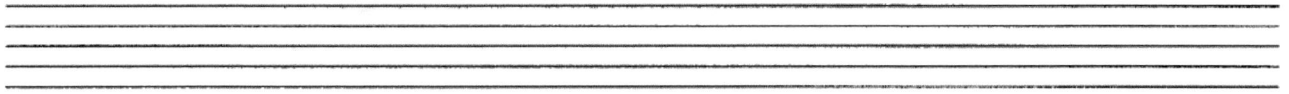

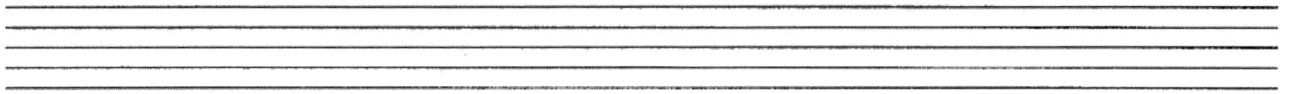

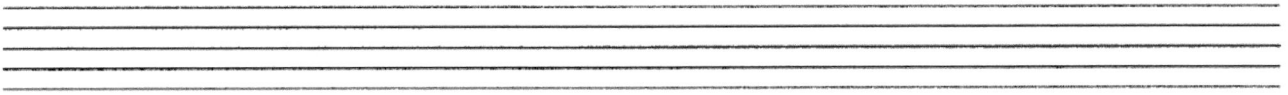

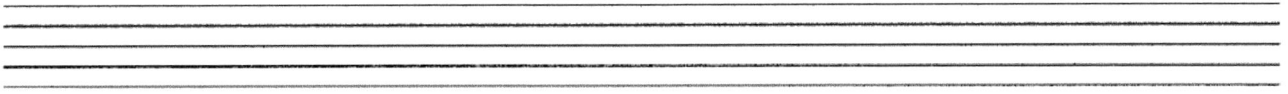

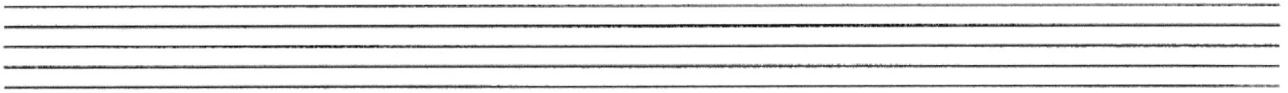

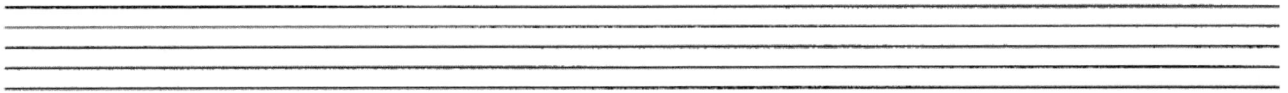

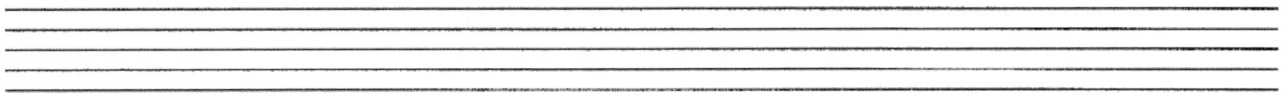

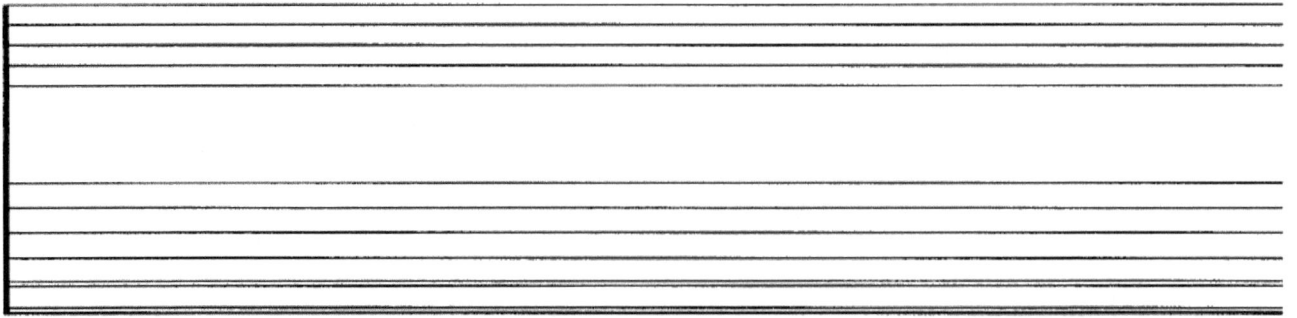

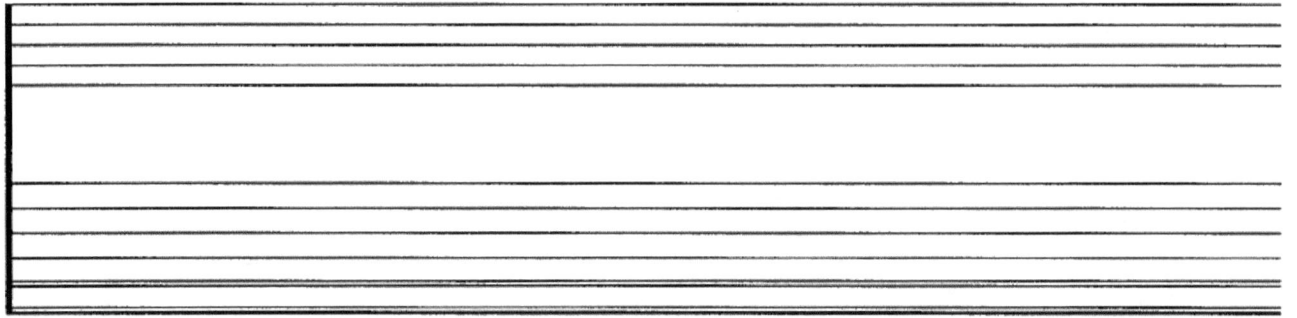

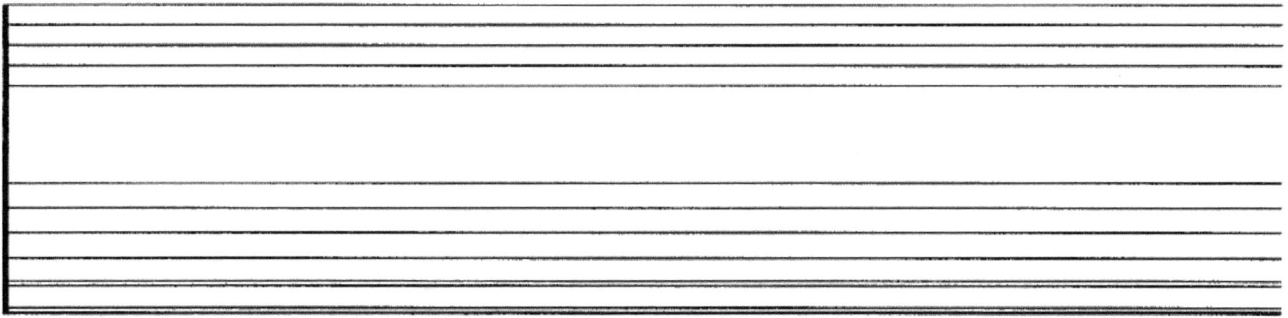

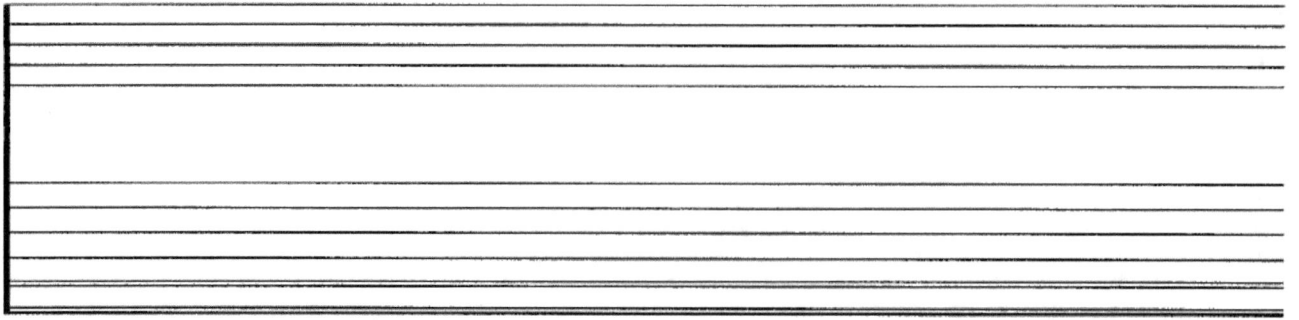

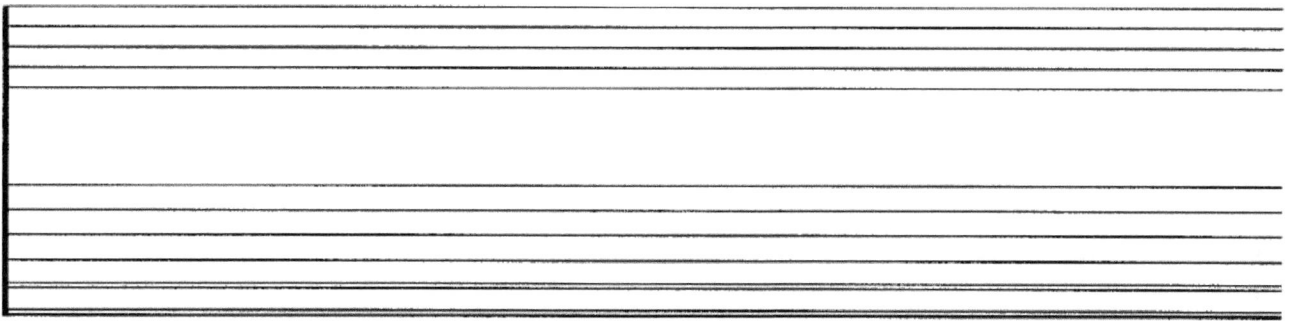

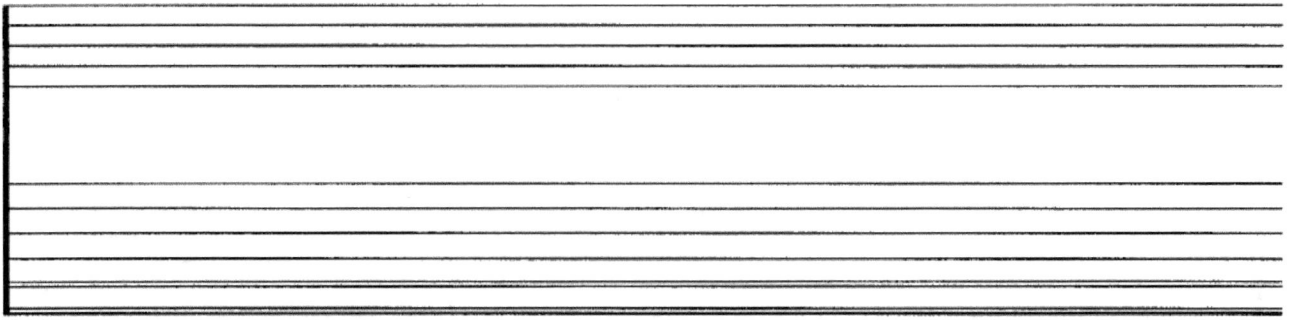

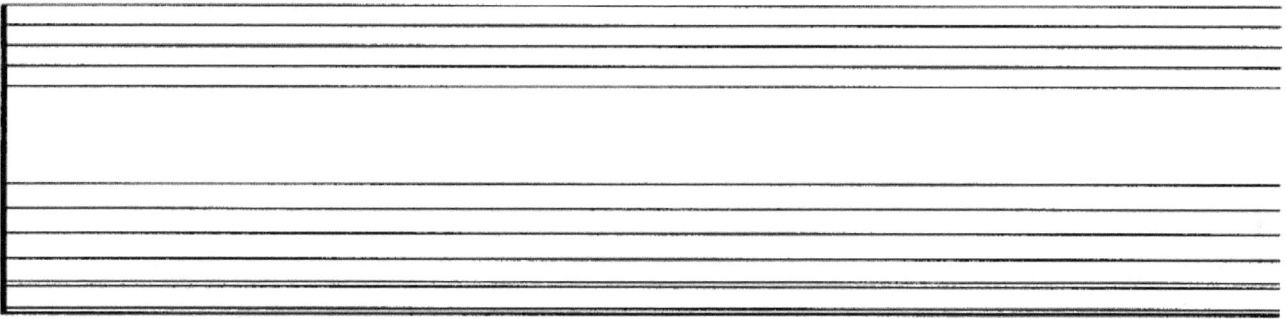

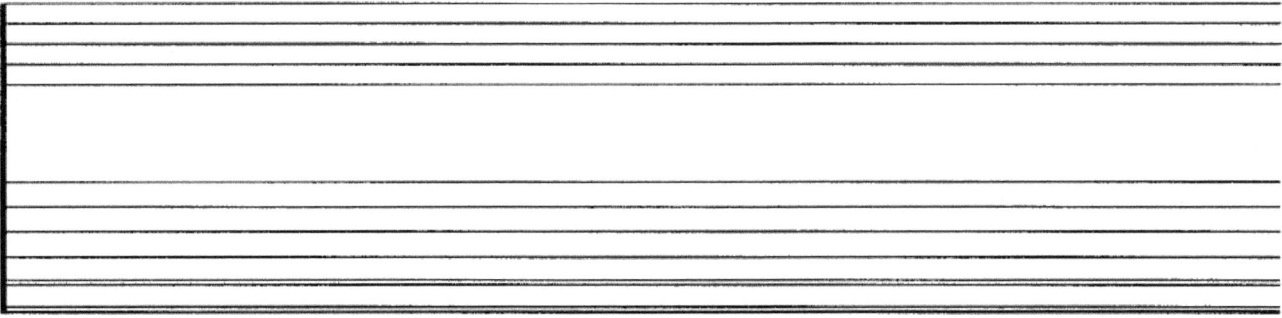

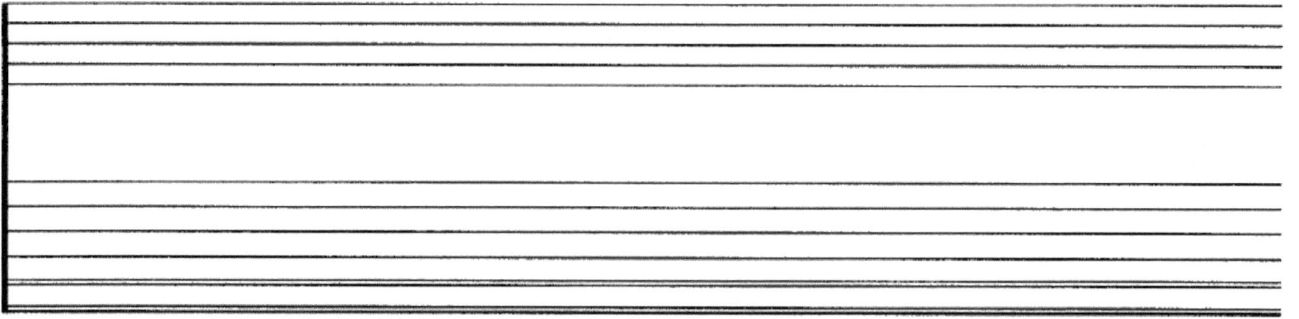

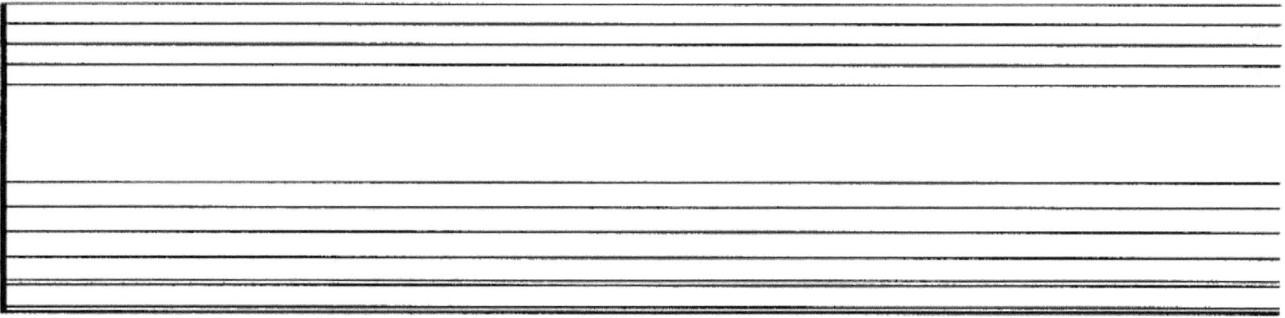

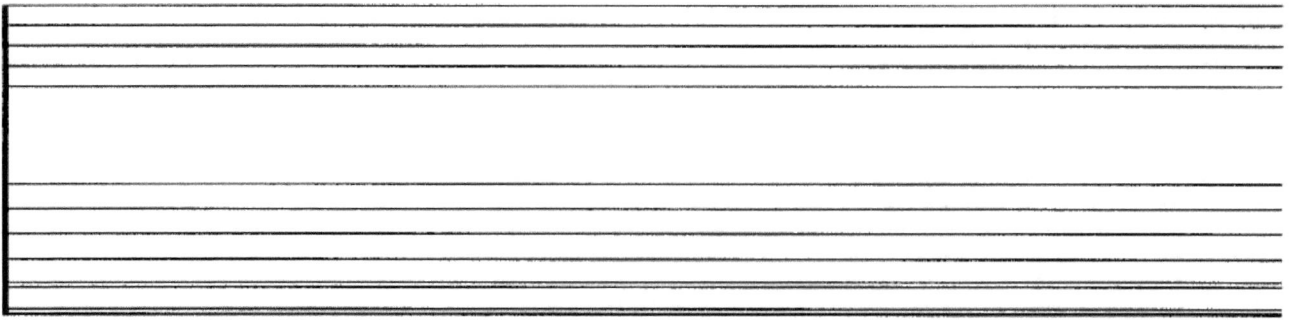

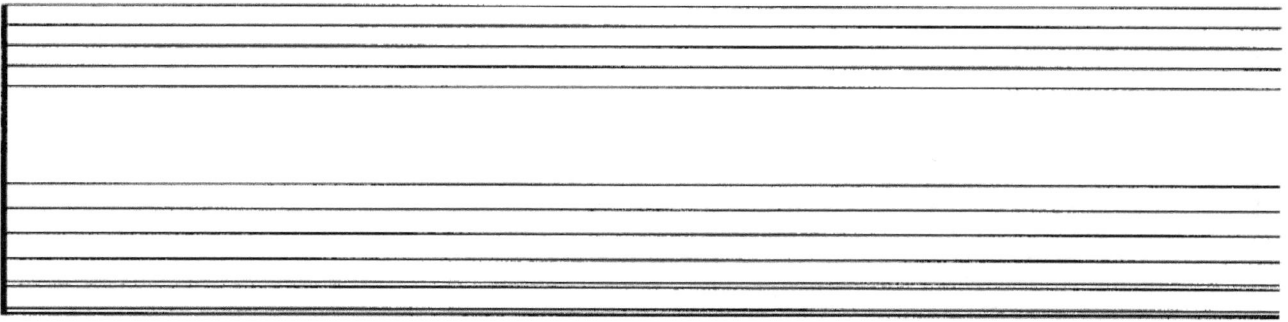

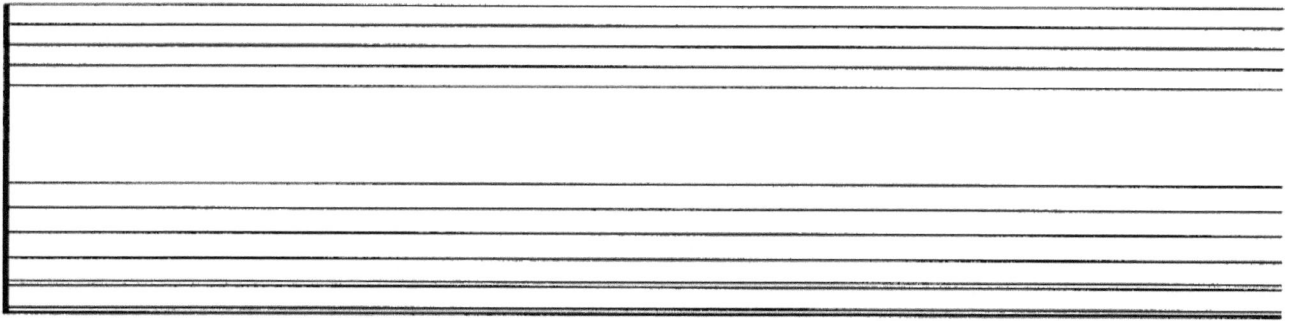

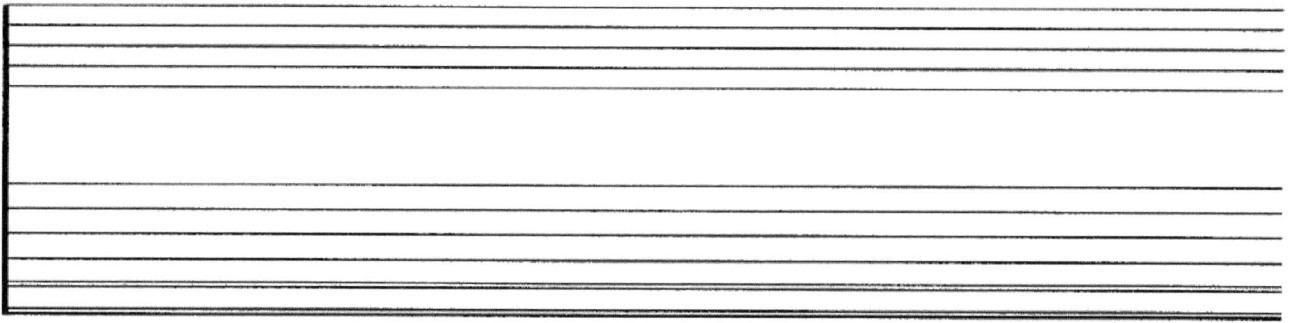

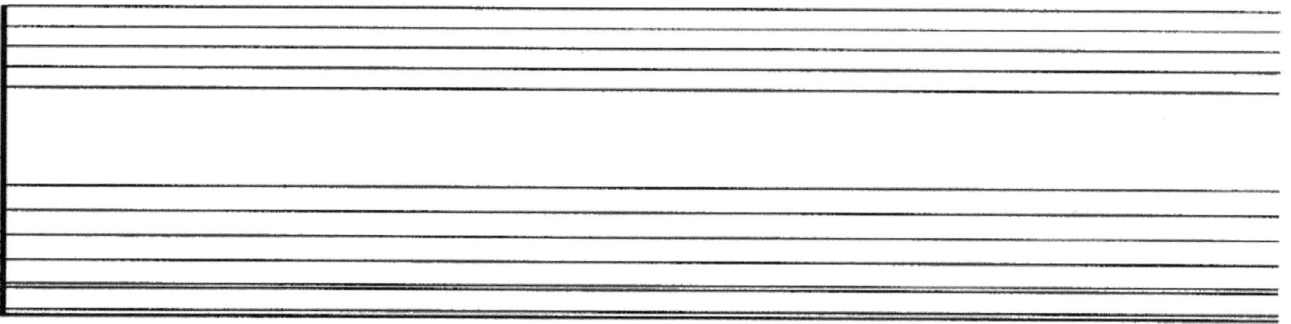

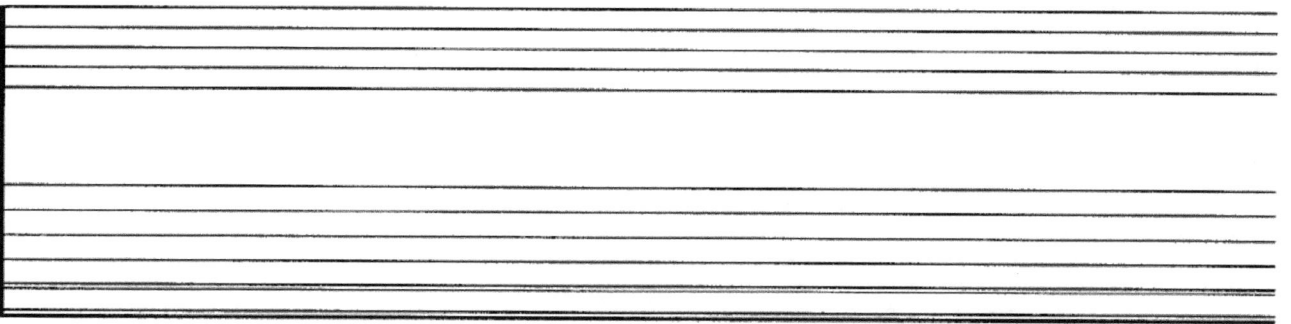

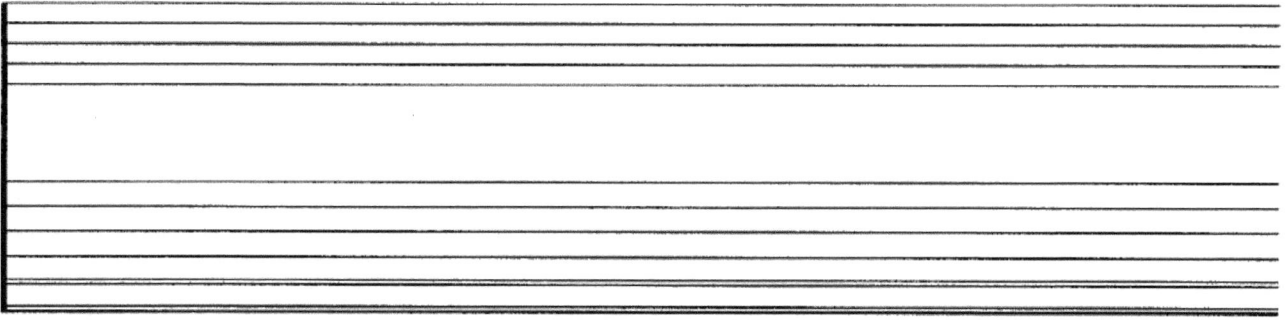

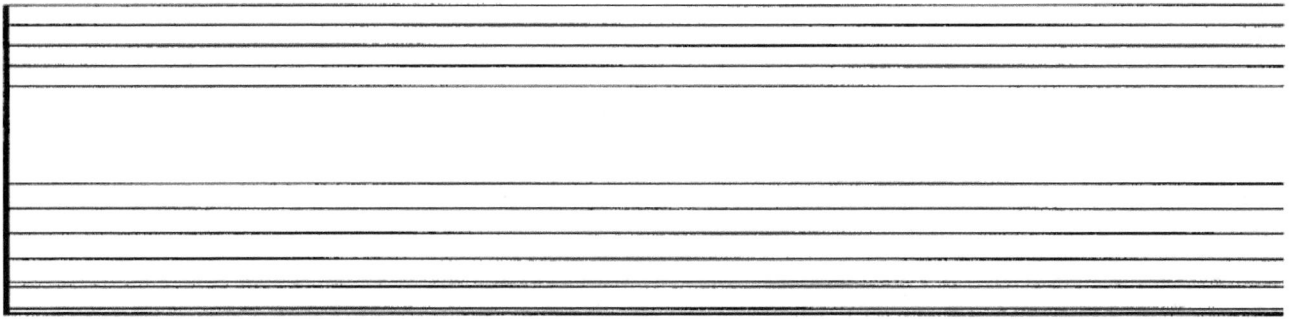

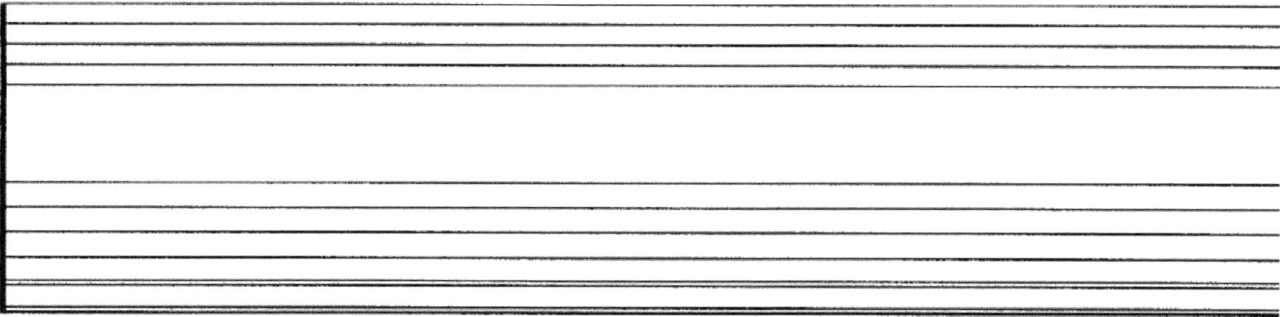

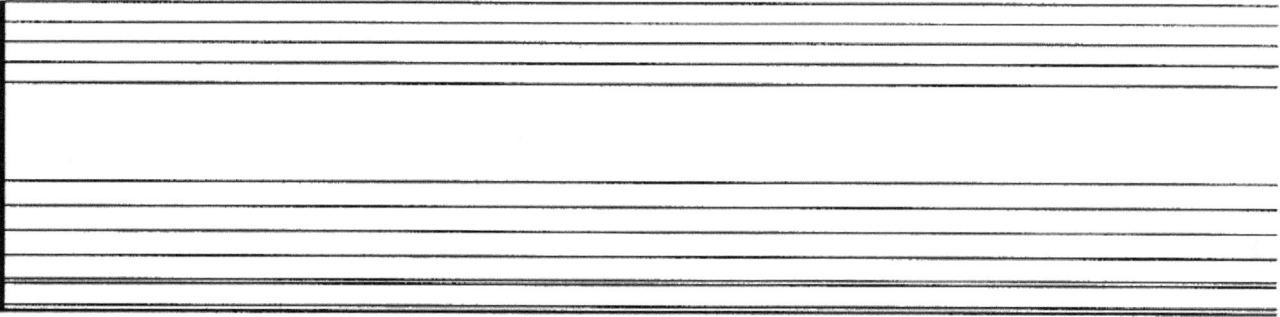

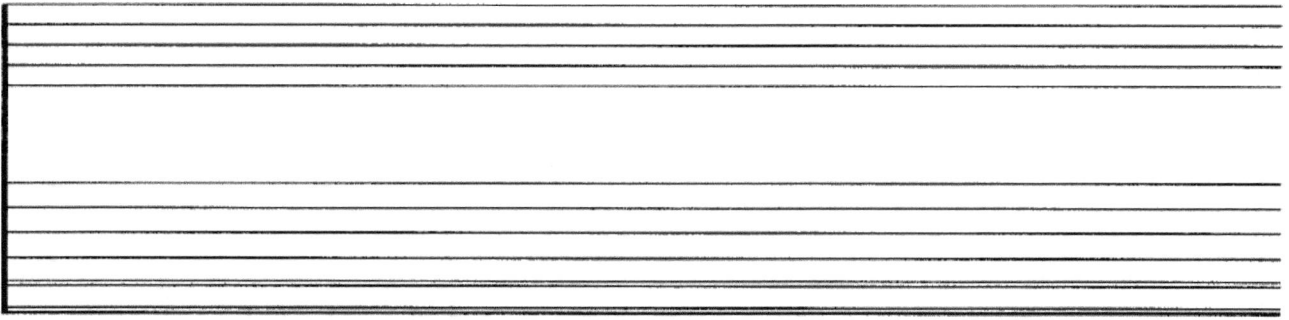

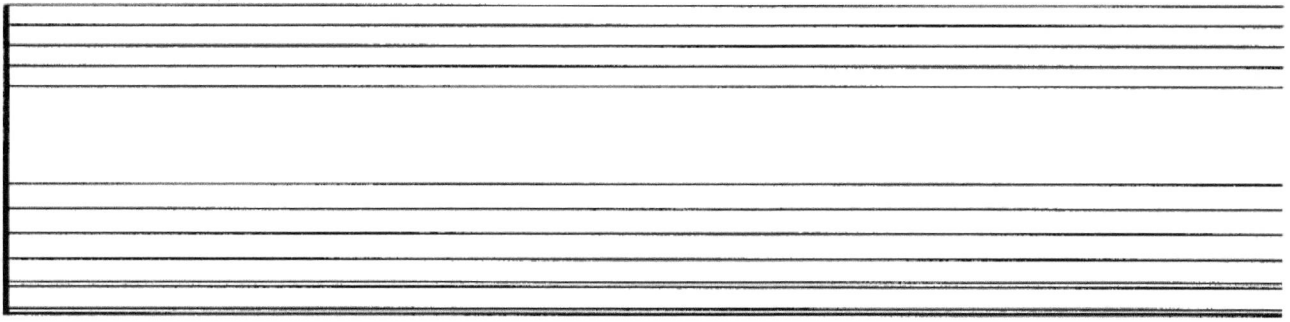

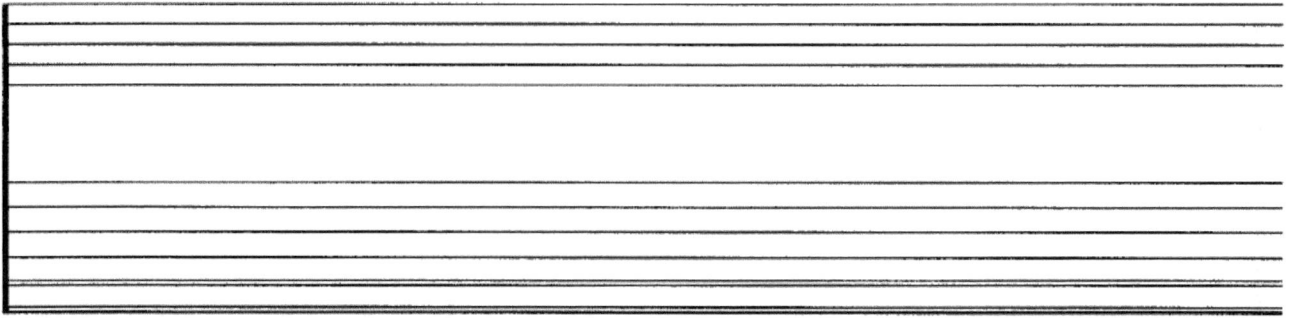

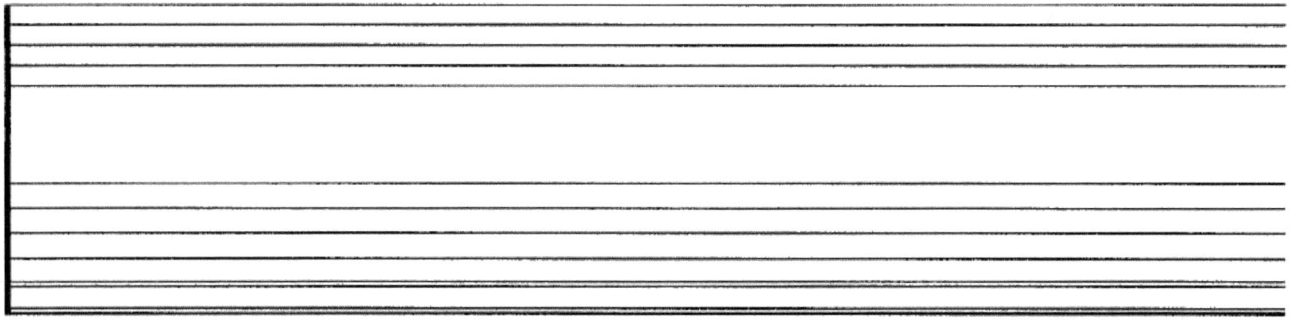

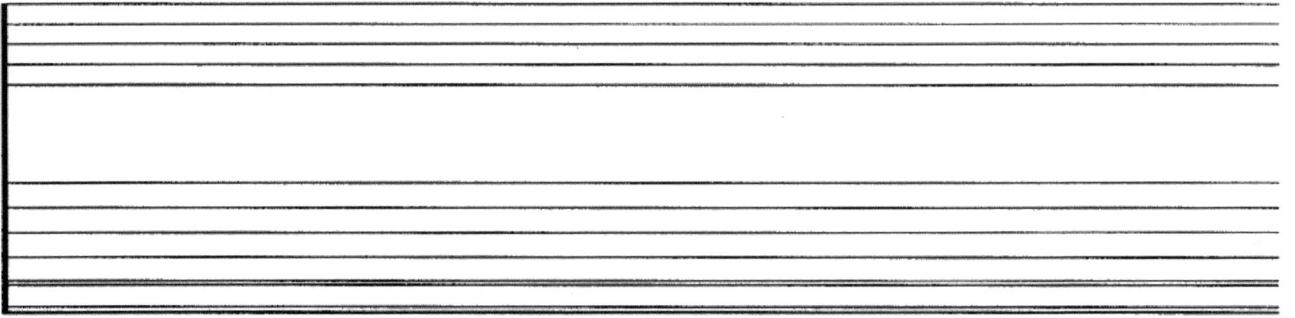

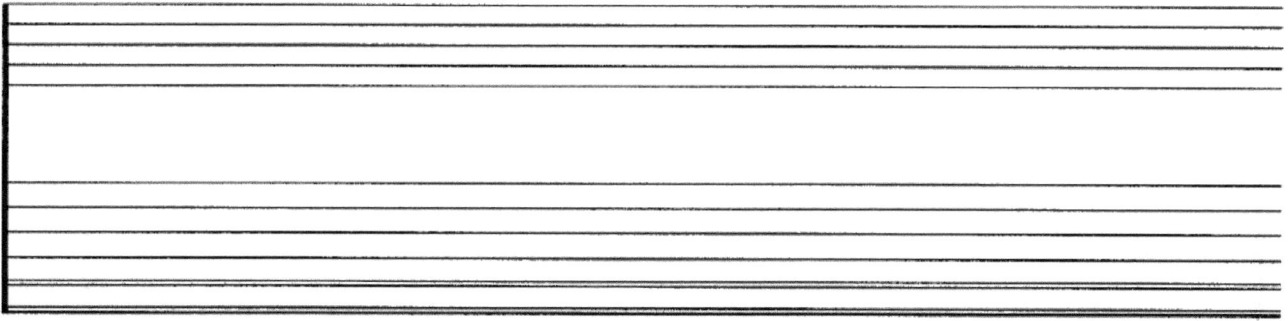

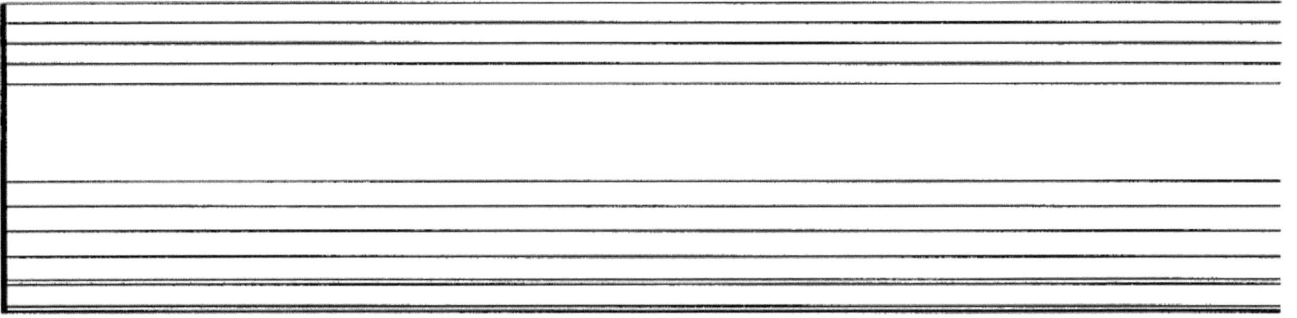

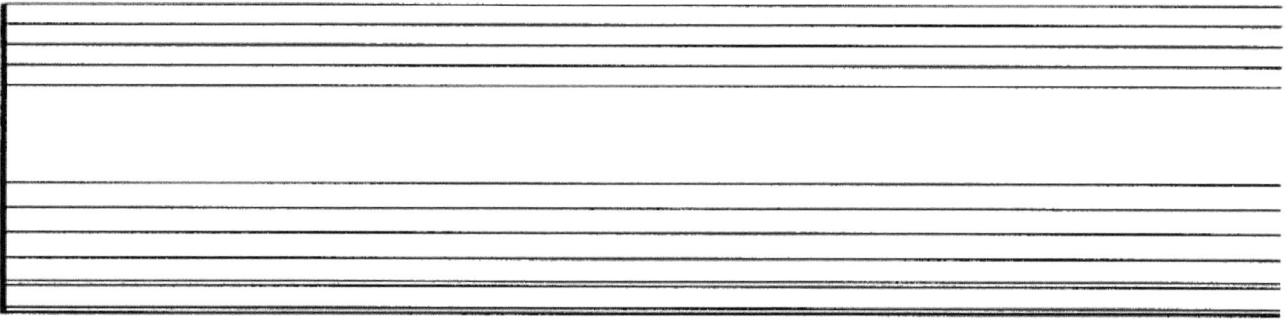

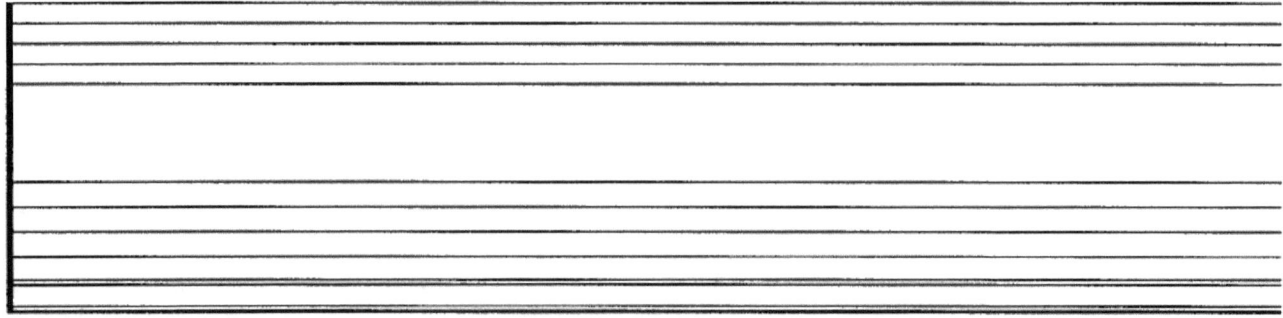

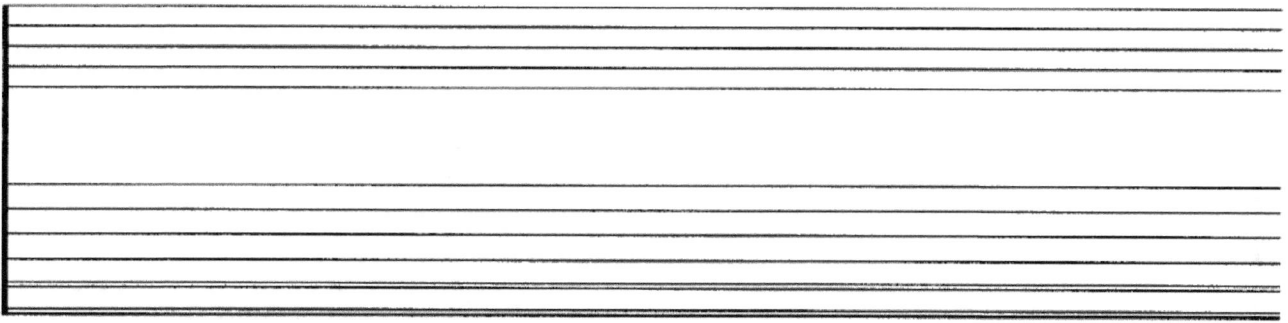

www.ingramcontent.com/pod-product-compliance
Lightning Source LLC
LaVergne TN
LVHW081316060426
835509LV00015B/1549